MONTY PYTHON AND THE HOLY GRAIL

Other books by Monty Python

A Pocketful of Python – Picked by Michael Palin
A Pocketful of Python – Picked by Terry Jones
A Pocketful of Python – Picked by John Cleese
A Pocketful of Python – Picked by Terry Gilliam
A Pocketful of Python – Picked by Eric Idle
Monty Python's Big Red Book
The Brand New Monty Python Papperbok
Monty Python Scrapbook/The Life of Brian
Monty Python and the Holy Grail (Book)
Monty Python's The Meaning of Life
Monty Python's Flying Circus: Just the Words VOLUME ONE
Monty Python's Flying Circus: Just the Words VOLUME TWO
The Fairly Incomplete & Rather Badly Illustrated Monty
    Python Songbook
The Life of Brian Screenplay

MONTY PYTHON AND THE HOLY GRAIL

Screenplay by
John Cleese, Graham Chapman
Terry Gilliam, Eric Idle
Terry Jones, Michael Palin

Methuen

1 3 5 7 9 10 8 6 4 2

This promotional edition published by Methuen 2003

Methuen Publishing Limited
215 Vauxhall Bridge Road, London SW1V 1EJ

Copyright © 1974 Python (Monty) Pictures Ltd
Photographs by Drew Mara

Methuen Publishing Limited Reg. No. 3543167

ISBN 0 413 77394 9

Typeset by SX Composing DTP, Rayleigh, Essex
Printed and bound in Great Britain
by Cox & Wyman Ltd, Reading, Berkshire

PYTHON (MONTY) PICTURES LTD
in association with
MICHAEL WHITE
presents

MONTY PYTHON
and
THE HOLY GRAIL

Mønti Pythøn lk den Hølie Gräilen

Written and performed by:
GRAHAM CHAPMAN
JOHN CLEESE
ERIC IDLE
TERRY GILLIAM
TERRY JONES
MICHAEL PALIN

Røtern nik Akten Di

with
CONNIE BOOTH
CAROL CLEVELAND
NEIL INNES
BEE DUFFELL
JOHN YOUNG
RITA DAVIES

Wik

Also appearing
AVRIL STEWART
SALLY KINGHORN

Alsø wik

Also also appearing

MARK ZYCON	ELSPETH CAMERON
MITSUKO FORSTATER	SANDY JOHNSON
SANDY ROSE	ROMILLY SQUIRE
JONI FLYNN	ALISON WALKER
LORAINE WARD	ANNA LANSKI
SALLY COOMBE	VIVIENNE MACDONALD
YVONNE DICK	DAPHNE DARLING
FIONA GORDON	GLORIA GRAHAM
JUDY LAMS	TRACY SNEDDON
SYLVIA TAYLOR	JOYCE POLLNER

MARY ALLEN

Alsø alsø wik

Camera Operator	HOWARD ATHERTON
Camera Focus	JOHN WELLARD
Camera Assistant	ROGER PRATT
Camera Grip	RAY HALL
Chargehand Electrician	TERRY HUNT
Lighting	TELEFILM LIGHTING SERVICE LTD
	ANDREW RITCHIE AND SON LTD
	TECHNICOLOR
Rostrum Cameraman	KENT HOUSTON

Wi nøt trei a høliday in Sweden this yër?

Sound Recordist	GARTH MARSHALL
Sound Mixer	HUGH STRAIN

Boom Swinger	GODFREY KIRBY
Sound Maintenance	PHILIP CHUBB
Sound Assistant	ROBERT DOYLE
Dubbing Editor	JOHN FOSTER
Assistant Editors	JOHN MISTER, NICK GASTER, ALEXANDER CAMPBELL ASKEW, BRIAN PEACHEY, DANIELLE KOCHAVI
Sound Effects	IAN CRAFFORD

See the løveli lakes

Continuity	PENNY EYLES
Accountant	BRIAN BROCKWELL
Production Secretary	CHRISTINE WATT
Property Buyer	BRIAN WINTERBORN
Property Master	TOM RAEBURN
Property Men	ROY CANNON, CHARLIE TORBETT, MIKE KENNEDY
Catering	RON HELLARD LTD
Vehicles	BUDGET RENT-A-CAR LTD

The wøndërful telephøne system

Assistant Art Director	PHILIP COWLAM
Construction Manager	BILL HARMAN
Carpenters	NOBBY CLARK, BOB DEVINE
Painter	GRAHAM BULLOCK
Stagehand	JIM N. SAVERY
Rigger	ED SULLIVAN

And mani interesting furry animals

With special extra thanks to
Charlie Knode, Brian McNulty, John Gledhill, Peter
Thomson, Sue Cable, Valerie Charlton, Drew Mara, Sue
Smith, Charlie Coulter, Iain Monaghan, Steve Bennell,
Bernard Belenger, Alpini McAlpine, Hugh Boyle, Dave
Taylor, Gary Cooper, Peter Saunders, Les Shepherd,
Vaughn Millard, Hamish MacInnes, Terry Mosaic, Bawn
O'Beirne Ranelagh

Made entirely on location in Scotland at Doune Castle,
Castle Stalker, Killin, Glen Coe, Arnhall Castle, Bracklim
Falls, Sherriffmuir

By Python (Monty) Pictures Ltd, 20 Fitzroy Square,
London W1, England
And completed at Twickenham Film Studios, England
Copyright © 1974 National Film Trustee Company Ltd.
All Rights Reserved

The Producers would like to thank the Forestry
Commission, Doune Admissions Ltd, Keir and Cawdor
Estates, Stirling University, and the people of Doune for
their help in the making of this film

Songs
NEIL INNES

Additional music
DEWOLFE

A møøse once bit my sister . . .

Costume Designer
HAZEL PETHIG

No realli! She was Karving her initials on the møøse with the
sharpened end of an interspace tøøthbrush given her by
Svenge – her brother-in-law – an Oslo dentist and star of
many Norwegian møvies: 'The Høt Hands of an Oslo
Dentist', 'Fillings of Passion', 'The Huge Mølars of Horst
Nordfink'.

We apologise for the fault in the subtitles. Those responsible
have been sacked.

Mynd you, møøse bites Kan be pretty nasti . . .

We apologise again for the fault in the subtitles. Those
responsible for sacking the people who have just been sacked
have been sacked.

Production Manager	JULIAN DOYLE
Assistant Director	GERRY HARRISON
Special Effects	JOHN HORTON
Fight Director &	
Period Consultant	JOHN WALLER

Make-up Artists	PEARL RASHBASS, PAM LUKE
Special Effects Photography	JULIAN DOYLE
Animation Assistance	LUCINDA COWELL, KATE HEPBURN
Møøse trained by	TUTTE HERMSGER-VØRDENBRØTBØRDA
Lighting Cameraman	TERRY BEDFORD
Special Møøse Effects	OLAF PROT
Møøse Costumes	SIGGI CHURCHILL
Designer	ROY SMITH
Møøse Choreographed by	HORST PROT III
Miss Taylor's Møøses by	HENGST DOUGLAS-HOME
Møøse trained to mix concrete and sign complicated insurance forms by	JURGEN WIGG
Editor	JOHN HACKNEY
Møøses' noses wiped by	BJORN IRKESTOM-SLATER WALKER
Large møøse on the left half side of the screen in the third scene from the end, given a thorough grounding in Latin, French and O Level Geography by	BO BENN
Suggestive poses for the Møøse suggested by	VIC ROTTER
Antler-care by	LIV THATCHER

The directors of the firm hired to continue the credits after the other people had been sacked, wish it to be known that they have just been sacked.

The credits have been completed in an entirely different style at great expense and at the last minute.

TITLE ON YELLOW B.G.
Executive Producer
JOHN GOLDSTONE & 'RALPH' The Wonder Llama

Producer
MARK FORSTATER

Assisted by
EARL J. LLAMA
MIKE Q. LLAMA III
SY LLAMA
MERLE Z. LLAMA IX

Directed by
40 SPECIALLY TRAINED
ECUADORIAN MOUNTAIN LLAMAS
6 VENEZUELAN RED LLAMAS
142 MEXICAN WHOOPING LLAMAS
14 NORTH CHILEAN GUANACOS
(CLOSELY RELATED TO THE LLAMA)
REG LLAMA OF BRIXTON
76,000 BATTERY LLAMAS
FROM 'LLAMA-FRESH' FARMS LTD, NEAR
PARAGUAY
and
TERRY GILLIAM and TERRY JONES

1. EXT. CASTLE WALLS. DAY.

*Mist. Several seconds of it swirling about. Silence. Possibly,
atmospheric music. Superimpose 'England AD 787'. After a few
more seconds we hear hoofbeats in the distance. They come slowly
closer. Then out of the mist comes* KING ARTHUR *followed by a*
SERVANT *who is banging two halves of coconuts together.*
ARTHUR *raises his hand.*

ARTHUR: Whoa there!

> SERVANT *makes noises of horses halting, with a flourish.*
> ARTHUR *peers through the mist. Cut to shot from over his
> shoulder: castle (e.g. Bodium) rising out of the mist. On the
> castle battlements a* SOLDIER *is dimly seen. He peers down.*

SOLDIER: Halt! Who goes there!

ARTHUR: It is I, Arthur, son of Uther Pendragon, from the
Castle of Camelot, King of all Britons, defeater of the
Saxons, Sovereign of all England.

> *Pause.*

SOLDIER: Get away!

ARTHUR: I am . . . And this is my trusty servant, Patsy. We
have ridden the length and breadth of the land in search
of Knights who will join our Court at Camelot. I must
speak with your lord and master.

SOLDIER: What? Ridden on a horse?

ARTHUR: Yes.

SOLDIER: You're using coconuts.

ARTHUR: . . . What?

SOLDIER: You're using two empty halves of coconuts and
banging them together.

ARTHUR (*scornfully*): So? We have ridden since the snows of
winter covered this land, through the Kingdom of Mercia.

1

SOLDIER: Where did you get the coconuts?

ARTHUR: Through . . . we found them.

SOLDIER: Found them? In Mercia. The coconut's tropical.

ARTHUR: What do you mean?

SOLDIER: Well, this is a temperate zone.

ARTHUR: The swallow may fly south with the sun, or the
house martin or the plover seek hot lands in winter, yet
these are not strangers to our land.

A moment's pause.

SOLDIER: Are you suggesting coconuts migrate?

ARTHUR: Not at all. They could be carried.

SOLDIER: What? A *swallow* carrying a *coconut*?

ARTHUR: It could grip it by the husk . . .

SOLDIER: It's not a question of where he grips it, it's a simple
matter of weight – ratios . . . a five-ounce bird could not
hold a one-pound coconut.

ARTHUR: Well, it doesn't matter. Go and tell your master
that Arthur from the Court of Camelot is here.

A slight pause. Swirling mist. Silence.

SOLDIER: Look! To maintain velocity a swallow needs to
beat its wings four hundred and ninety-three times every
second. Right?

ARTHUR (*irritated*): Please!

SOLDIER: Am I right?

ARTHUR: I'm not interested.

SECOND SOLDIER (*who has loomed up on the battlements*): It
could be carried by an African swallow.

FIRST SOLDIER: Oh yes! An African swallow maybe . . . but
not by a European swallow. That's *my* point.

SECOND SOLDIER: Oh yes, I agree there . . .

ARTHUR (*losing patience*): Will you *ask* your master if he
wants to join the Knights of Camelot?

FIRST SOLDIER: But then of course African swallows are
non-migratory.

SECOND SOLDIER: Oh yes.

> ARTHUR *raises his eyes heavenwards and nods to* PATSY.
> *They turn and go off into the mist.*

FIRST SOLDIER: So they wouldn't be able to bring a coconut back anyway.

> *The* SOLDIERS' *voices recede behind them.*

SECOND SOLDIER: Wait a minute! Suppose two swallows carried it together?

FIRST SOLDIER: No, they'd have to have it on a line.

> *Stillness. Silence again.*

2. ANIMATION/LIVE-ACTION SEQUENCE – DEATH AND DEVASTATION.

Cut to Terry Gilliam's sequence of Brueghel prints. Sounds of strange medieval music. Discordant and sparse. Wailings and groanings. The last picture mixes through into live action. Big close-up of contorted face upside down. A leg falls across it. Creaking noise. The bodies lurch away from camera to reveal they are amongst a huge pile of bodies on a swaying cart that is lumbering away from camera. It is pulled by a couple of ragged, dirty, emaciated WRETCHES. *Behind the cart walks another* MAN *who looks slightly more prosperous, but only on the scale of complete and utter impoverishment. He wears a black hood and looks sinister.*

CART DRIVER: Bring out your dead!

> *We follow the cart through a wretched, impoverished plague-ridden village. A few starved mongrels run about in the mud scavenging. In the open doorway of one house perhaps we just glimpse a pair of legs dangling from the ceiling. In another doorway an* OLD WOMAN *is beating a cat against a wall rather like one does with a mat. The cart passes round a dead donkey or cow in the mud. And a* MAN *tied to a cart is being hammered to death by four* NUNS *with huge mallets.*

CART DRIVER: Bring out your dead!

There are legs sticking out of windows and doors. Two MEN *are fighting in the mud – covered from head to foot in it. Another* MAN *is on his hands and knees shovelling mud into his mouth. We just catch sight of a* MAN *falling into a well.*

CART DRIVER: Bring out your dead!

Some PEASANTS *drag a body up to the cart. It stops. They load the body on to the cart and the* CART DRIVER *receives some payment. Further down the road a* LARGE MAN *comes out of a house and the cart stops again. The* LARGE MAN *is carrying the* BODY *of an old man by the scruff of the neck and seat of the pants.*

CART DRIVER: Bring out your dead!

LARGE MAN: Here's one!

CART DRIVER: Ninepence.

BODY: I'm not dead.

CART DRIVER: What?

LARGE MAN: Nothing. There's your ninepence.

BODY: I'm not dead.

CART DRIVER: 'Ere. He says he's not dead.

LARGE MAN: Yes he is.

BODY: I'm not.

CART DRIVER: He isn't.

LARGE MAN: He will be soon. He's very ill.

BODY: I'm getting better.

LARGE MAN: You're not. You'll be stone dead in a few minutes.

CART DRIVER: I can't take him like this. It's against regulations.

BODY: I don't want to go on the cart.

LARGE MAN: Don't be such a baby.

CART DRIVER: I can't take him.

BODY: I feel fine.

LARGE MAN: Do me a favour.

CART DRIVER: I can't.

4

LARGE MAN: Well, can you hang around a couple of
minutes? He won't be long.

CART DRIVER: I promised I'd be at the Robinsons'. They've
lost nine today.

LARGE MAN: When's your next round?

CART DRIVER: Thursday.

BODY: I think I'll go for a walk.

LARGE MAN: You're not fooling anyone, you know. (*To*
CART DRIVER.) Isn't there anything you could do?

BODY: (*singing unrecognisably*) I feel happy, I feel happy.

The CART DRIVER *looks at the* LARGE MAN *for a moment.*
Then they both do a quick furtive look up and down the
street. The CART DRIVER *very swiftly brings up a club and*
hits the BODY. *(Out of shot but the singing stops after a loud*
bonk noise.)

LARGE MAN (*handing over the money at last*): Thanks very
much.

CART DRIVER: That's all right. See you Thursday.

They turn . . . Suddenly all in the village fall to their knees,
touching forelocks etc. ARTHUR *and* PATSY *ride into shot,*
slightly nose in air, they ride through without acknowledging
anybody. After they pass, the LARGE MAN *turns to the*
CART DRIVER.

LARGE MAN: Who's that then?

CART DRIVER (*grudgingly*): I dunno, must be a king.

LARGE MAN: Why?

CART DRIVER: He hasn't got shit all over him.

3. EXT. DAY.

ARTHUR *and* PATSY *riding. They stop and look. We see a castle*
in the distance, and before it a PEASANT *is working away on his*
knees trying to dig the earth with his bare hands and a twig.
ARTHUR *and* PATSY *ride up, and stop before the* PEASANT.

5

ARTHUR: Old woman!

DENNIS (*turning*): Man.

ARTHUR: Man. I'm sorry. Old man, what knight lives in that castle?

DENNIS: I'm thirty-seven.

ARTHUR: What?

DENNIS: I'm only thirty-seven . . . I'm not *old*.

ARTHUR: Well – I can't just say: 'Hey, Man!'

DENNIS: You could say: 'Dennis'.

ARTHUR: I didn't know you were called Dennis.

DENNIS: You didn't bother to find out, did you?

ARTHUR: I've said I'm sorry about the old woman, but from behind you looked . . .

DENNIS: What I object to is that you automatically treat me as an inferior . . .

ARTHUR: Well . . . I *am* King.

DENNIS: Oh, very nice. King, eh! I expect you've got a palace and fine clothes and courtiers and plenty of food. And how d'you get that? By exploiting the workers! By hanging on to outdated imperialistic dogma, which perpetuates the social and economic differences in our society! If there's *ever* going to be any progress . . .

An OLD WOMAN *appears.*

OLD WOMAN: Dennis! There's some lovely filth down here . . . Oh! How d'you do?

ARTHUR: How d'you do, good lady . . . I am Arthur, King of the Britons . . . can you tell me who lives in that castle?

OLD WOMAN: King of the *who*?

ARTHUR: The Britons.

OLD WOMAN: Who are the Britons?

ARTHUR: All of us . . . we are all Britons.

DENNIS *winks at the* OLD WOMAN.

ARTHUR: . . . And I am your King . . .

OLD WOMAN: Ooooh! I didn't know we had a king. I thought we were an autonomous collective . . .

DENNIS: You're fooling yourself. We're living in a dictatorship, a self-perpetuating autocracy in which the working classes . . .

OLD WOMAN: There you are, bringing class into it again . . .

DENNIS: That's what it's all about . . . If only –

ARTHUR: Please, please, good people, I am in haste. What knight lives in that castle?

OLD WOMAN: No one lives there.

ARTHUR: Well, who is your lord?

OLD WOMAN: We don't have a lord.

ARTHUR: What?

DENNIS: I told you, we're an anarcho-syndicalist commune, we take it in turns to act as a sort of executive officer for the week.

ARTHUR: Yes . . .

DENNIS: . . . But all the decisions of that officer . . .

ARTHUR: Yes, I see.

DENNIS: . . . must be approved at a bi-weekly meeting by a simple majority in the case of purely internal affairs.

ARTHUR: Be quiet.

DENNIS: . . . But a two-thirds majority . . .

ARTHUR: Be quiet! I order you to shut up.

OLD WOMAN: Order, eh? Who does he think he is?

ARTHUR: I am your King.

OLD WOMAN: Well, I didn't vote for you.

ARTHUR: You don't vote for kings.

OLD WOMAN: Well, how did you become King, then?

ARTHUR: The Lady of the Lake, her arm clad in purest shimmering samite, held Excalibur aloft from the bosom of the waters to signify that by Divine Providence . . . I, Arthur, was to carry Excalibur . . . that is why I am your King.

DENNIS: Look, strange women lying on their backs in ponds handing over swords . . . that's no basis for a system of government. Supreme executive power derives from a mandate from the masses not from some farcical aquatic ceremony.

ARTHUR: Be quiet!

DENNIS: You can't expect to wield supreme executive power just because some watery tart threw a sword at you.

ARTHUR: Shut up!

DENNIS: I mean, if I went round saying I was an emperor because some moistened bint had lobbed a scimitar at *me*, people would put me away.

ARTHUR (*grabbing him by the collar*): Shut up, will you. Shut up!

DENNIS: Ah! *Now* . . . we see the violence inherent in the system.

ARTHUR: Shut up!

PEOPLE (*i.e. other* PEASANTS*) are appearing and watching.*

DENNIS (*calling*): Come and see the violence inherent in the system. Help, help, I'm being repressed!

ARTHUR (*aware that people are now coming out and watching*): Bloody peasant! (*Pushes* DENNIS *over into the mud and prepares to ride off.*)

DENNIS: Oooooh! Did you hear that! What a give-away.

ARTHUR: Come on, Patsy.

They ride off.

DENNIS (*in background as we pull out*): Did you see him repressing me, then? That's what I've been on about . . .

4. EXT. FOREST. DAY.
Mix through to ARTHUR *and* PATSY *riding through the forest. They pass rune stones. We track with them. Close-ups of their faces as they ride. Mix to another tracking shot of them riding*

9

through the forest. They come to a clearing and stop, looking ahead intently. Their eyes light up.

Sound FX of fight.

Cut to their eyeline. A clearing on the other side of which is a rough wooden footbridge across a stream. At the start of the bridge a tremendous fight is going on. A huge BLACK KNIGHT *in black armour, his face totally masked in a visor, is fighting a slightly smaller* KNIGHT *in green armour. (Perhaps the* GREEN KNIGHT*'s armour is identical to the* BLACK KNIGHT*'s save for the colour.)*

Cut back to ARTHUR *and* PATSY. *They watch, growing more impressed as they watch the fight.*

Cut back to the fight. The GREEN KNIGHT *lunges at the* BLACK KNIGHT, *who avoids the blow with a skilful side-step and parry, knocking the sword out of the* GREEN KNIGHT*'s hand.*

Cut back to ARTHUR *and* PATSY *even more impressed.*

Cut back to the fight. The GREEN KNIGHT *has drawn out a particularly nasty mace or spiked ball and chain, much longer than the* BLACK KNIGHT*'s sword.*

ARTHUR *narrows his eyes, wondering whether the* BLACK KNIGHT *will survive.*

Cut back to the fight. The GREEN KNIGHT *swings at the* BLACK KNIGHT, *who ducks under the first swing, leaps over the second and starts to close on the* GREEN KNIGHT.

Cut back to ARTHUR *and* PATSY *watching like a tennis match. Sound FX of the fight reaching a climax. Four almighty clangs. Then silence.*

Cut back to see the GREEN KNIGHT *stretched out. The* BLACK KNIGHT *sheathes his sword.*

ARTHUR *looks at* PATSY. *Nods and they move forward.*

Cut back to the BLACK KNIGHT *picking up the* GREEN KNIGHT *above his head and hurling him into the river.* ARTHUR *and* PATSY *approach him.*

ARTHUR: You fight with the strength of many men, Sir Knight.

The BLACK KNIGHT *stares impassively and says nothing.*

ARTHUR: I am Arthur, King of the Britons.

Hint of a pause as he waits for a reaction which doesn't come. ARTHUR *is only slightly thrown.*

. . . I seek the bravest and the finest knights in all the world to join me in my Court at Camelot . . .

The BLACK KNIGHT *remains silent.*

ARTHUR: You have proved yourself worthy. . . . Will you join me?

Silence.

ARTHUR: You make me sad. But so be it. Come, Patsy.

As he moves, the BLACK KNIGHT *bars the way.*

BLACK KNIGHT: None shall pass.

ARTHUR: What?

BLACK KNIGHT: None shall pass.

ARTHUR: I have no quarrel with you, brave Sir Knight, but I must cross this bridge.

BLACK KNIGHT: Then you shall die.

ARTHUR: I command you, as King of the Britons, to stand aside.

BLACK KNIGHT: I move for no man.

ARTHUR: So be it.

ARTHUR *draws his sword and approaches the* BLACK KNIGHT. *A furious fight now starts lasting about fifteen seconds at which point* ARTHUR *delivers a mighty blow which completely severs the* BLACK KNIGHT'*s left arm at the shoulder.* ARTHUR *steps back triumphantly.*

ARTHUR: Now stand aside, worthy adversary.

BLACK KNIGHT (*glancing at his shoulder*): 'Tis just a scratch.

ARTHUR: A scratch? Your arm's off.

BLACK KNIGHT: No it isn't.

ARTHUR (*pointing to the arm on ground*): What's that then?

BLACK KNIGHT: I've had worse.

ARTHUR: You're a liar.

BLACK KNIGHT: Come on, you pansy.

Another ten seconds furious fighting till ARTHUR *chops the* BLACK KNIGHT'*s other arm off, also at the shoulder. The arm, plus sword, lies on the ground.*

ARTHUR: Victory is mine. (*Sinking to his knees.*) I thank thee O Lord that in thy . . .

BLACK KNIGHT: Come on then.

ARTHUR: What!

He kicks ARTHUR *hard on the side of his helmet.* ARTHUR *gets up, still holding his sword. The* BLACK KNIGHT *comes after him, kicking.*

ARTHUR: You are indeed brave, Sir Knight, but the fight is mine.

BLACK KNIGHT: Had enough?

ARTHUR: You stupid bastard. You haven't got any arms left.

BLACK KNIGHT: Course I have.

ARTHUR: Look!

BLACK KNIGHT: What! Just a flesh wound. (*Kicks* ARTHUR.)

ARTHUR: Stop that.

BLACK KNIGHT (*kicking him*): Had enough . . . ?

ARTHUR: I'll have your leg.

He is kicked.

Right!

The BLACK KNIGHT *kicks him again and* ARTHUR *chops his leg off. The* BLACK KNIGHT *keeps his balance with difficulty.*

BLACK KNIGHT: I'll do you for that.

ARTHUR: You'll what . . . ?

BLACK KNIGHT: Come here.

ARTHUR: What are you going to do. Bleed on me?

BLACK KNIGHT: I am invincible.

ARTHUR: You're a loony.

BLACK KNIGHT: The Black Knight always triumphs. Have at you!

ARTHUR *takes his last leg off. The* BLACK KNIGHT*'s body lands upright.*

BLACK KNIGHT: All right, we'll call it a draw.

ARTHUR: Come, Patsy.

    ARTHUR *and* PATSY *start to cross the bridge.*

BLACK KNIGHT: Running away, eh? You yellow bastard, come back here and take what's coming to you. I'll bite your legs off!

5. EXT. DAY.

A village. Sound of chanting of Latin canon, punctuated by short, sharp cracks. It comes nearer. We see it is a line of MONKS *à la* Seventh Seal *flagellation scene, chanting and banging themselves on the foreheads with wooden boards. They pass a group of villagers who are dragging a beautiful* YOUNG WOMAN *dressed as a witch through the streets. They drag her to a strange house/ruin standing on a hill outside the village. A strange-looking knight stands outside,* SIR BEDEVERE.

FIRST VILLAGER: We have found a witch. May we burn her?

ALL: A witch! Burn her!

BEDEVERE: How do you know she is a witch?

ALL: She looks like one. Yes, she does.

BEDEVERE: Bring her forward.

    They bring her forward – a beautiful YOUNG GIRL (MISS ISLINGTON) *dressed up as a witch.*

WITCH: I am not a witch. I am not a witch.

BEDEVERE: But you are dressed as one.

WITCH: They dressed me up like this.

ALL: We didn't, we didn't!

WITCH: This is not my nose. It is a false one.

    BEDEVERE *takes her nose off.*

BEDEVERE: Well?

FIRST VILLAGER: . . . Well, we did do the nose.

BEDEVERE: The nose?

FIRST VILLAGER: And the hat. But she is a witch.

ALL: A witch, a witch, burn her!

BEDEVERE: Did you dress her up like this?

FIRST VILLAGER: . . . Um . . . Yes . . . no . . . a bit . . . yes . . .
she has got a wart.

BEDEVERE: Why do you think she is a witch?

SECOND VILLAGER: She turned *me* into a newt.

BEDEVERE: A newt?

SECOND VILLAGER (*after looking at himself for some time*): I
got better.

ALL: Burn her anyway.

BEDEVERE: Quiet! Quiet! There are ways of telling whether
she is a witch.

ARTHUR *and* PATSY *ride up at this point and watch what
follows with interest.*

ALL: There are? Tell us. What are they, wise Sir Bedevere?

THIRD VILLAGER: Do they hurt?

BEDEVERE: Tell me . . . what do you do with witches?

ALL: Burn them.

BEDEVERE: And what do you burn, apart from witches?

FOURTH VILLAGER: . . . Wood?

BEDEVERE: So why do witches burn?

SECOND VILLAGER (*pianissimo*): . . . Because they're made
of wood?

BEDEVERE: Good.

PEASANTS *stir uneasily then come round to this conclusion.*

ALL: I see. Yes, of course.

BEDEVERE: So how can we tell if she is made of wood?

FIRST VILLAGER: Make a bridge out of her.

BEDEVERE: Ah . . . but can you not also make bridges out of
stone?

ALL: Ah. Yes, of course . . . um . . . er . . .

17

BEDEVERE: Does wood sink in water?

ALL: No, no, it floats. Throw her in the pond. Tie weights on her. To the pond.

BEDEVERE: Wait. Wait . . . tell me, what also floats on water?

ALL: Bread? No, no, no. Apples . . . gravy . . . very small rocks . . .

BEDEVERE: No, no, no.

ARTHUR: A duck!

They all turn and look at ARTHUR. BEDEVERE *looks up very impressed.*

BEDEVERE: Exactly. So . . . logically . . .

FIRST VILLAGER (*beginning to pick up the thread*): If she . . . weighs the same as a duck . . . she's made of wood.

BEDEVERE: And therefore?

ALL: A witch! . . . A duck! A duck! Fetch a duck.

FOURTH VILLAGER: Here is a duck, Sir Bedevere.

BEDEVERE: We shall use my largest scales.

He leads them a few yards to a very strange contraption indeed, made of wood and rope and leather. They put the GIRL *in one pan and the duck in another. Each pan is supported by a wooden stave.* BEDEVERE *checks each pan then . . .* ARTHUR *looks on with interest.*

BEDEVERE: Remove the supports.

Two PEASANTS *knock them away with sledgehammers. The* GIRL *and the duck swing slightly but balance perfectly.*

ALL: A witch! A witch!

WITCH: It's a fair cop.

ALL: Burn her! Burn her! Let's make her into a ladder.

The VILLAGERS *drag the girl away, leaving* ARTHUR *and* BEDEVERE *regarding each other admiringly.*

BEDEVERE: Who are you who are so wise in the ways of science?

ARTHUR: I am Arthur, King of the Britons.

BEDEVERE *immediately drops to his knees.*

BEDEVERE: My Liege . . . forgive me . . .

ARTHUR looks at PATSY with obvious satisfaction.

ARTHUR: Good Sir Knight, will you come with me to Camelot and join our number at the Round Table?

BEDEVERE: My Liege, I am honoured.

ARTHUR steps forward, drawing his sword, with a slight hint of difficulty.

ARTHUR: What is your name?

BEDEVERE: Bedevere, my Liege.

ARTHUR: Then I dub you . . . *Sir* Bedevere . . . Knight of the Round Table!

Heroic music as we mix through to a close-up of a book on which is written:

6. THE BOOK OF THE FILM

VOICE-OVER: The wise Sir Bedevere was the first to join King Arthur's Knights . . . but other illustrious names were soon to follow . . .

Hand turns page.

VOICE: Sir Lancelot the Brave . . .

Hand turns page.

VOICE: Sir Galahad the Pure . . .

Hand turns page.

VOICE: And Sir Robin-the-not-quite-so-pure-as-Sir-Lancelot . . .

Hand turns page.

VOICE: . . . who had nearly fought the Dragon of Angnor . . .

Hand turns page.

VOICE: . . . who had nearly stood up to the vicious Chicken of Bristol . . .

Hand turns page.

VOICE: . . . and who had personally wet himself at the Battle of Badon Hill . . . and the aptly named . . .

Hand turns page.

VOICE: Sir Not-Appearing-In-This-Film

Hand turns page.

VOICE: Together they formed a band whose names and
deeds were to be retold throughout the centuries . . . The
Knights of the Round Table . . .

A gorilla's hand snatches away the hand.

Music swells and fades and we mix through to:

7. EXT. SUNSET.

Fairly close head-on shot of the KNIGHTS *riding along.*
BEDEVERE *and* ARTHUR *at the front of the group deep in*
conversation.

BEDEVERE: And that, my Lord, is how we know the Earth to
be banana-shaped.

ARTHUR: This new learning amazes me, Sir Bedevere.
Explain again how sheep's bladders may be employed to
prevent earthquakes.

BEDEVERE: Of course, my Liege . . .

LAUNCELOT (*he points*): Look, my Liege!

They all stop and look.

ARTHUR (*with thankful reverence*): Camelot!

Cut to shot of amazing castle in the distance. Illuminated in
the rays of the setting sun.

Music.

Cut back to ARTHUR *and the group. They are all staring*
with fascination.

GALAHAD: Camelot . . .

LAUNCELOT: Camelot . . .

GAWAIN (*at the back, to* PAGE): It's only a model.

ARTHUR (*turning sharply*): Sh! (*To the rest.*) Knights! I bid you
welcome to your new home! Let us ride . . . to Camelot!

Cut to interior of medieval hall. A large group of armoured KNIGHTS *are engaged in a well-choreographed song-and-dance routine of the very up-beat 'If they could see me now' type of fast bouncy number. The poorer verses are made clearer by cutting to a group of* KNIGHTS *actually engaged in the described task while the line itself is sung. They sing:*

KNIGHTS We're Knights of the Round Table
　　　　We dance whene'er we're able
　　　　We do routines and chorus scenes
　　　　With footwork impeccable
　　　　We dine well here in Camelot
　　　　We eat ham and jam and Spam a lot.

　　　　We're Knights of the Round Table
　　　　Our shows are formidable
　　　　But many times
　　　　We're given rhymes
　　　　That are quite unsingable
　　　　We're opera mad in Camelot
　　　　We sing from the diaphragm a lot.

　　　　Booming basses. A routine where two XYLOPHONISTS *play parts of* KNIGHTS' *armour producing a pleasing effect.*

KNIGHTS: In war we're tough and able,
　　　　Quite indefatigable
　　　　Between our quests
　　　　We sequin vests
　　　　And impersonate Clark Gable
　　　　It's a busy life in Camelot.

SINGLE MAN: I have to push the pram a lot.

　　　　Cut back to ARTHUR *and* BEDEVERE *and* COMPANY *as we had left them.*

ARTHUR: No, on second thoughts let's not go to Camelot.

KNIGHTS: Right!

ARTHUR: It is a silly place.

> *They set off again and almost immediately they are suffused in an ethereal radiance and strange heavenly choir music. The* PAGES, *horselike, take fright for a moment, they whinny and rattle their coconuts.* ARTHUR *and the* KNIGHTS *fall on their knees. A holy voice booms out.*

GOD: Arthur! Arthur . . . King of the Britons . . .

> *They all prostrate themselves even further.*

Oh, don't grovel . . . do get up! If there's one thing I can't stand it's people grovelling!!

> ARTHUR *and* COMPANY *rise.*

ARTHUR: Sorry . . .

GOD: And don't apologise. Every time I try to talk to someone it's sorry this and forgive me that and I'm not worthy and . . . just stand there. What are you doing now?

ARTHUR: I'm averting my eyes, Lord.

GOD: Well, don't. It's like those miserable psalms. They're so depressing. Now knock it off.

ARTHUR: Yes, Lord.

GOD: Right. Arthur, King of the Britons, your knights of the Round Table shall have a task to make them an example in these dark times . . .

ARTHUR: Good idea, O Lord.

GOD: Course it's a good idea.

> *Suddenly another light glows beside* GOD *or possibly within the light which is* GOD *a shape slowly starts to form.*

Behold . . . Arthur . . . this is the Holy Grail . . .

> *The form in the bright light is just discernible as an iridescent chalice . . . the* KNIGHTS *gasp.*

Look well, Arthur . . . for it is your sacred task to seek this Grail . . .

> *It begins to fade. Music crescendo as both lights fade.*

> . . . that is your purpose Arthur . . . the Quest for the
> Holy Grail . . .

It is gone. All the KNIGHTS *are left gasping in awe and
wonderment. They all turn and look at* ARTHUR.

LAUNCELOT: A blessing. A blessing from the Lord.

GALAHAD: God be praised!

Stirring music crescendo. They ride off.

*Cut to titles sequence. Animation: 'The Quest for the Holy
Grail'. After titles cut to:*

9. EXT. CASTLE. DAY.

*Mix through one or two shots of them on their way again, until
they approach a terrific castle (a little one would do too). They
advance quite close to the castle and draw themselves into a line.
At a signal from* ARTHUR *two* PAGES *step forward and give a
brief fanfare.*

A MAN *appears on the battlements.* ARTHUR *addresses him.*

ARTHUR: Hello.

MAN: 'Allo. Whoo is eet?

ARTHUR: I am King Arthur and these are my Knights of the
Round Table. Whose castle is this?

MAN: This is the castle of my master, Guy de Loimbard.

ARTHUR: Please go and tell your master that we have been
charged by God with a sacred quest, and if he will give
us food and shelter this night he may join us in our quest
for the Holy Grail.

MAN: Well, I'll ask him, but I don't think he'll be very keen.
He's already got one, you see.

ARTHUR: What?

GALAHAD: He says they've already got one.

They are stunned.

ARTHUR: Are you sure he's got one?

24

MAN: Oh yes. It's very nice.

Cut to battlements. The TAUNTER (MAN) *turns to some others:*

MAN: I told them we already got one.

They all giggle.

ARTHUR: Well . . . can we come up and have a look?

MAN: Of course not. You are English pigs.

ARTHUR: Well, what are you, then?

MAN: I'm French. Why do you think I have this outrageous accent, you silly King.

GALAHAD: What are you doing in England?

MAN: Mind your own business.

ARTHUR: If you will not show us the Grail we shall storm your castle.

Murmurs of assent.

MAN: You don't frighten us, English pig-dog. Go and boil your bottom, son of a silly person. I blow my nose on you so-called Arthur King, you and your silly English k . . . niggets.

He puts hands to his ears and blows a raspberry.

GALAHAD: What a strange person.

ARTHUR: Now look here, my good man.

MAN: I don't want to talk to you, no more, you empty-headed animal food trough wiper. I fart in your general direction. Your mother was a hamster and your father smelled of elderberries.

GALAHAD: Is there someone else up there we could talk to?

MAN: No. Now go away or I shall taunt you a second time.

ARTHUR: Now this is your last chance. I've been more than reasonab . . .

Cut back to battlements.

MAN: Fetchez la vache!

SOLDIER: Quoi?

MAN: Fetchez la vache!

A cow is led out of a stall.

Cut back to ARTHUR.

ARTHUR: Now that is my final offer. If you are not prepared to agree to my demands, I shall be forced to take . . . Oh Christ!

A cow comes flying over the battlements, lowing aggressively. The cow lands on GALAHAD'S PAGE, *squashing him completely.*

ARTHUR: Right! Knights! Forward!

ARTHUR *leads a charge towards the castle. Various shots of them battling on, despite being hit by a variety of farm animals.*

ARTHUR (*as the* MAN *next to him is squashed by a sheep*): Knights! Run away!

Midst echoing shouts of 'run away' the KNIGHTS *retreat to cover with the odd cow or goose hitting them still. The* KNIGHTS *crouch down under cover.*

LAUNCELOT: The sods! I'll tear them apart.

ARTHUR (*restraining* LAUNCELOT *from going out and having a go*): No!

BEDEVERE: I have a plan, sir.

Cut back to battlements of a castle. FRENCH SENTRIES *suspiciously peering towards the English lines. Wind whistles.*

Shot of the empty scrubland or undergrowth or woodland around the castle. Emptiness. Wind. More shots of the FRENCH SENTRIES *peering into the dusk.*

During all this the sounds of extensive carpentry have possibly been heard, followed by silence, followed by renewed outbursts of activity.

Close-up on FRENCH *looking very nervous. Dawn breaking. Shot of woodland. Nothing. Wind. Dawn still breaking. Shots of the* FRENCH. *They suddenly hear something. A faintly detectable squeaking which is getting louder.*

Cut to wide shot of castle and woodland. Squeaking getting louder. Shot of the CHIEF TAUNTER *pointing. Wide shot again. The squeaking gets louder and an enormous twenty-foot-high wooden rabbit is wheeled out of the undergrowth into the open space in front of the castle. The* ENGLISH *scuttle back into the undergrowth. The rabbit has a large red bow tied round it and a rather crudely written label, which reads 'Pour votres amis Francais'. The* CHIEF TAUNTER *looks at it, narrowing his eyes. Then he turns and leaves battlements.*

Cut to ARTHUR *and* COMPANY *watching from the bushes. The main gate of the castle opens a little and the* CHIEF TAUNTER's *head sticks out, then another Froggie head, then another. They mutter to each other in French, look rather pleased, then rush out and start to pull the giant rabbit in.*

Cut back to ARTHUR *and* COMPANY *behind some bushes watching.*

ARTHUR: Now what happens?

BEDEVERE: Well now, Launcelot, Galahad and I wait until nightfall and then leap out of the rabbit and take the French by surprise, not only by surprise but totally unarmed and . . .

ARTHUR: Who . . . Who breaks out?

BEDEVERE: Er . . . we . . . Launcelot, Galahad and I . . . er . . . leap out of the rabbit and . . .

LAUNCELOT *covers his eyes.*

BEDEVERE: . . . Look, if we were to build a large wooden badger . . .

ARTHUR *cuffs him.* ARTHUR *looks at the battlements. There is a loud twang. Look of horror. The rabbit comes sailing over the battlements.*

ARTHUR: Run away!

More shouts.

Run away!

They continue to retreat. The rabbit lands on GAWAIN'S
PAGE *(who is already weighed down by enormous quantity
of luggage).*

10. EXT. CASTLE WALLS. DAY.
Cut to a MAN *in modern dress standing outside a castle. He
speaks straight to camera in a documentary kind of way.
Superimpose caption: 'A Very Famous Historian'.*

HISTORIAN'S SPEECH: Defeat at the castle seems to have
    utterly disheartened King Arthur . . . The ferocity of the
    French taunting took him completely by surprise and
    Arthur became convinced that a new strategy was
    required if the Quest for the Holy Grail were to be
    brought to a successful conclusion. Arthur, having
    consulted his closest Knights, decided that they should
    separate and search for the Grail individually. This now
    is what they did. No sooner . . .

    A KNIGHT *rides into shot and hacks him to the ground. He
    rides off.*

        We stay for a moment on the glade. A MIDDLE-AGED
    LADY *in a C&A twin-set emerges from the trees and looks
    in horror at the body of her* HUSBAND.
MRS HISTORIAN: Frank!

    *Cut to animated frame, with the words 'The Tale of Sir
    Robin' on it. Pleasant pastoral music. Mix through to:*
VOICE: The Tale of Sir Robin.

11. EXT. GLADE. DAY.
A KNIGHT *is trotting along through a wooden sun-dappled glade,
followed by his trusty* PAGE *banging the usual half coconuts. As*

29

we see them approach we hear the beautiful lilting sound of medieval music, and see that the KNIGHT *is followed by a small retinue of* MUSICIANS *in thirteenth-century courtly costume, one sings, and plays the tambourine, one bangs at a tabor (a small drum* OED*) and one plays upon the pipes.*

The KNIGHT *looks very proud and firm as we hear the first part of the song, but the combination of the lyrics and the large signs they pass, start to have their effect . . .*

SONG: Bravely good Sir Robin, rode forth from Camelot,
    He was not afraid to die, oh brave Sir Robin,
    He was not at all afraid to be killed in nasty ways
    Brave brave brave brave Sir Robin.

    He was not in the least bit scared to be mashed into a
      pulp
    And have his eyes gouged out and his elbows broken;
    To have his kneecaps split and his body burned away
    And his limbs all hacked and mangled, brave Sir Robin.

    His head smashed in, and his heart gouged out,
    And his liver removed, and his bowels unplugged,
    And his nostrils raped, and his bottom burned off,
    And his penis split . . . and his . . .
ROBIN: Er, that's . . . That's enough music for a while, lads.
    It looks as though there's dirty work afoot.
SINGERS: Brave, Sir Rob . . .
ROBIN: Shut up.

    They have ridden past the following signs, all in triplicate:—

CAMELOT 43	CERTAIN DEATH 1
CAMELOT 43	CERTAIN DEATH 1
CAMELOT 43	CERTAIN DEATH 1

BEWARE   GO BACK   DEAD PEOPLE ONLY
BEWARE   GO BACK   DEAD PEOPLE ONLY
BEWARE   GO BACK   DEAD PEOPLE ONLY

12. EXT. GLADE. DAY.

They now pass three KNIGHTS *impaled to a tree. With their feet off the ground, with one lance through the lot of them, they are skewered up like a barbecue.*

Then they pass three KNIGHTS *sitting on the ground with one enormous axe through their skulls. They look timorous.*

SIR ROBIN *rides on a little way with the music building up enormous and terrifying tension, until suddenly there standing before him is an enormous* THREE-HEADED KNIGHT.

Large terrifying chord.

(Incidentally the three heads come out of one large body, specially built to accommodate three actors, although the KNIGHT *has the usual complement of arms and legs. The* THREE HEADS *of the* KNIGHT *speak in unison.)*

THREE HEADS: Halt! Who art thou?
SINGERS: He is brave Sir Robin, brave Sir Robin, who . . .
ROBIN (*to* SINGERS): Shut up. Oh, nobody really. Just
    passing through.
THREE HEADS: What do you want?
SINGERS: To fight and . . .
ROBIN: Shut up. Nothing really. Just to pass through, good
    Sir Knight. I am a Knight of King Arthur's Round Table.
THREE HEADS: You are a Knight of the Round Table?
ROBIN: I am.

From now on the THREE HEADS *speak individually.*
SECOND HEAD: Shit.
FIRST HEAD: In that case I shall have to kill you.
SECOND HEAD: Shall I?

THIRD HEAD: Oh, I don't think so.

SECOND HEAD: I'm not sure.

THIRD HEAD (*to* FIRST): What do *I* think?

FIRST HEAD: I think kill him.

THIRD HEAD: Oh! let's be nice to him.

FIRST HEAD: Oh! shut up!

ROBIN: Perhaps I could . . .

FIRST HEAD: Oh! quick! get the sword out – I want to cut his head off.

THIRD HEAD: Oh! cut your own head off.

SECOND HEAD: Yes – do us all a favour.

FIRST HEAD: What?

THIRD HEAD: Yapping on all the time.

SECOND HEAD: You're lucky, you're not next to him.

FIRST HEAD: What do you mean?

SECOND HEAD: You snore.

FIRST HEAD: Ooh, lies! Anyway, you've got bad breath.

SECOND HEAD: Well, only because you don't brush my teeth . . .

THIRD HEAD: Oh! Stop bickering and let's go and have tea and biscuits.

FIRST HEAD: All right! All right! We'll kill him first and then have the tea and biscuits.

SECOND HEAD: Yes.

THIRD HEAD: Oh! *not* biscuits . . .

FIRST HEAD: All right! All right! *not* biscuits – but let's kill him anyway . . .

Wide shot. The THREE-HEADED KNIGHT *is alone.*

SECOND HEAD: He's buggered off!

THIRD HEAD: So he has! He's scarpered!

13. EXT. GLADE. DAY.

Quick sequence of SIR ROBIN. *The music is jolly and bright, as if triumphant.* ROBIN *is not at all happy with the lyrics.*

SINGERS: Brave Sir Robin ran away.

ROBIN: I didn't.

SINGERS: Bravely ran away, away.

ROBIN: No, no, no.

SINGERS: When danger reared its ugly head
　　He bravely turned his tail and fled.
　　Yes, brave Sir Robin turned about
　　And gallantly he chickened out.
　　Bravely taking to his feet
　　He beat a very brave retreat.
　　Bravest of the brave Sir Robin
　　Petrified of being dead
　　Soiled his pants then brave Sir Robin
　　Turned away and fled.
　　They disappear into distance.
　　　Animation: 'The Tale of Sir Galahad'.

14. EXT. STORM. FOREST. DUSK.

As the storm rages we pick up GALAHAD *forcing his way through brambles and over slippery rocks. Progress is hard. He pauses and at this moment we hear the howling of wolves.* GALAHAD *turns, then hurries onward even more urgently. Another louder, closer howl is heard and* GALAHAD *stumbles and falls heavily. Though obviously injured he bravely struggles forward a little and regains his feet reacting with pain. More louder closer howling. He grips his sword valiantly and as he glances around a flash of lightning reveals the silhouette of a huge terrifying castle, perhaps looking rather derelict. He makes up his mind in an instant and stumbles manfully towards it. More louder howling. He reaches the forbidding and enormous doors of the castle and beats on the doors with the handle of his sword, looking over his shoulder the while. Pause. He beats again, shouting:*

GALAHAD: Open. Open the doors. In the name of King Arthur. Open the doors.

Some rattling chainy noises come from inside with huge bolts being drawn. The wolves' howling is very close. As the door creaks open GALAHAD steps quickly inside.

15. INT. CASTLE. NIGHT.

From inside we see GALAHAD enter, wiping the rain from his eyes, and turn as the door crashes behind him. GALAHAD turns to the door reacting to the fact he is trapped.

ZOOT (*out of vision*): Hello!

GALAHAD turns back. We see from his POV the lovely ZOOT standing by him smiling enchantingly and a number of equally delectable GIRLIES draped around in the seductively poulticed room. They look at him smilingly and wave.

GIRLIES: Hello!

ZOOT: Welcome, gentle Sir Knight, welcome to the Castle Anthrax.

GALAHAD: The Castle Anthrax?

ZOOT: Yes. It's not a very nice name, is it? But *we* are nice and will attend to your every . . . every need.

GALAHAD: Er . . . you are the keepers of the Holy Grail?

ZOOT: The what? . . . But you are tired and must rest awhile. Midget! Crapper!

ZOOT claps her hands. TWO stunning GIRLS run forward.

MIDGET AND CRAPPER: Yes, O Zoot?

ZOOT: Prepare a bed for our guest.

MIDGET AND CRAPPER (*grovelling with delight*): O thank you, Zoot, thank you, thank you.

ZOOT: Away varletesses! (*To GALAHAD.*) The beds here are warm and soft and very, very big.

GALAHAD: Well, look, er, I . . .

ZOOT: What is your name, handsome Knight?

GALAHAD: Er . . . Sir Galahad . . . the chaste.

ZOOT: Mine is Zoot. Just Zoot. (*She is very close to him for a moment.*) But come.

She turns away and leads him towards a door leading to a corridor leading to the bedchamber.

GALAHAD: Well, look, I'm afraid I really ought to be . . .

ZOOT: Sir Galahad!!

There is a gasp from the other GIRLS.

ZOOT: You would not be so ungallant as to refuse our hospitality.

GALAHAD *looks at the other* GIRLS. *They are clearly on the verge of being offended.*

GALAHAD: Well . . .

ZOOT (*she moves off and* GALAHAD *unwillingly follows*): I'm afraid our life must seem very dull and quiet compared with yours. We are but eightscore young blondes, all between sixteen and nineteen and a half, cut off in this castle, with no one to protect us. Oooh. It is a lonely life . . . bathing . . . dressing . . . undressing . . . making exciting underwear . . .

They reach the end of the corridor and enter the bedchamber. ZOOT *turns.*

ZOOT: We are not used to handsome knights . . . (*She notices him limping.*) But you are wounded!

GALAHAD: No, it's nothing.

ZOOT: You must see the doctors immediately. (*She claps again.*) You must lie down.

She almost forces him to lie on the bed as PIGLET *and* WINSTON *enter the room. They are equally beautiful and dressed exotically. They approach* GALAHAD.

PIGLET: Well, what seems to be the trouble?

GALAHAD: They're doctors?

ZOOT: They have a basic medical training, yes. Now you must try to rest. Dr Winston! Dr Piglet! Practise your art!!

ZOOT *leaves. The* DOCTORS *settle down next to* GALAHAD, *gaze into his eyes, and start to examine him, loosening his armour, and generally touching him in a just possibly medical way.* GALAHAD *is acutely uncomfortable, but does not like to say anything much . . .*

WINSTON: Try to *relax.*

GALAHAD: No, look, really, this isn't necess . . .

PIGLET: We must examine you.

GALAHAD: There's nothing wrong with . . . that.

PIGLET (*slightly irritated*): Please . . . we *are* doctors.

ZOOT *reappears.* GALAHAD *tries for one brief moment to relax. Then there is a sharp bong from the lower part of his armour.* WINSTON *glances quickly in the appropriate direction as* GALAHAD *sits up and starts getting off the bed and collecting his armour, saying:*

GALAHAD: No, no, this cannot be. I am sworn to chastity.

PIGLET: Back to your bed! At once!

GALAHAD: Torment me no longer! I have seen the Grail! I have seen it!

GALAHAD *hurries to the door and pushes through it. As he leaves the room we cut to the reverse to show that he is now in a room full of bathing and romping* GIRLIES, *all innocent, wide-eyed and beautiful. They smile enchantingly at him as he tries to keep walking without being too much diverted by the lovely sights assaulting his eyeballs. He nods to them stiffly once or twice and then his eye catches a particularly stunning* YOUNG LADY. *He visibly gulps with repressed emotion and then cannot resist saying:*

GALAHAD: Good evening . . . Ah, Zoot! Er . . .

DINGO: No, I am Zoot's identical twin sister, Dingo.

GALAHAD: Oh . . . will you excuse me?

DINGO: Where are you going?

GALAHAD: I have seen the Grail! I have seen it – here in this castle!

DINGO: No! Oh, no! Bad . . . *bad* Zoot!

GALAHAD: What is it?

DINGO: Bad, wicked, naughty Zoot . . . She has been setting fire to our beacon, which – I have just remembered – is Grail-shaped . . . this is not the first time we have had this problem.

GALAHAD: It's not the *real* Grail?

DINGO: Oh . . . wicked, *wicked* Zoot . . . she is a bad person and must pay the penalty. (*Turns to camera.*) Do you think this scene should have been cut? We were so worried when the boys were writing it but now we're glad. It's better than some of the previous scenes, I think.

Cut to:

THREE HEADS: At least ours was better, visually.

Cut to:

DENNIS: At least ours was committed. It wasn't just a string of pussy jokes.

Cut to:

BRIDGEKEEPER: Get on with it!

Cut to:

TIM: Get on with it!

DINGO (*to camera*): Oh, I am enjoying this scene.

Cut to:

GOD: Get on with it!

DINGO: Oh . . . wicked, *wicked* Zoot . . . she is a bad person and must pay the penalty. And here in Castle Anthrax we have but one punishment . . . you must tie her down on a bed . . . and spank her. Come!

DINGO *leads* GALAHAD *back into the bathing area by his hand.* GALAHAD *is by now so tempted and confused that he*

40

does not put up much physical resistance. The GIRLS *are*
shouting.

GIRLS: A spanking! A spanking!

DINGO: You must spank her well and when you have
spanked her you may deal with her as you like and
then . . . spank me.

AMAZING: And spank me!

STUNNER: And me.

LOVELY: And me.

DINGO: Yes. You must give us all a good spanking.

GIRLS: A spanking. A spanking. There is going to be a
spanking tonight.

DINGO: And after the spanking . . . the oral sex!

GALAHAD: Oh, dear! Well, I . . .

GIRLS: The oral sex . . . the oral sex.

GALAHAD: Well, I suppose I could stay a *bit* longer.
At this moment there is a commotion behind and SIR
LAUNCELOT *and* CONCORDE, *possibly plus* GAWAIN,
burst into the bathing area with swords drawn and form
themselves round SIR GALAHAD *threatening the* GIRLS.

LAUNCELOT: Sir Galahad!

GALAHAD: Oh . . . hello . . .

LAUNCELOT: Quick!

GALAHAD: Why?

LAUNCELOT: You are in great peril.

DINGO: No he isn't.

LAUNCELOT: Silence! foul temptress!
He threatens DINGO.

GALAHAD: Well, she's got a point.

LAUNCELOT: We'll cover your escape.

GALAHAD: Look – I'm fine.

GIRLS: Sir Galahad!

GALAHAD: No. Look, I can tackle this lot single-handed!

GIRLS: Yes, yes, let him tackle us single-handed!

LAUNCELOT: Come, Sir Galahad, quickly!

GALAHAD: No, really, I can cope. I can handle this lot easily.

GIRLS: Yes, let him handle us easily.

LAUNCELOT: No, sir. Quick!

He starts pulling GALAHAD *away.*

GALAHAD: No, please. Please! I can defeat them. There's only a hundred and fifty of them.

GIRLS: He will beat us easily. We haven't a chance.

By now LAUNCELOT *and* CONCORDE *have hustled* GALAHAD *out of the bathing area and are running through the outside door.*

LAUNCELOT: We were in the nick of time. You were in great peril.

GALAHAD (*dragging his feet somewhat*): I don't think I was.

LAUNCELOT: You were, Sir Galahad, you were in terrible peril.

GALAHAD: Look, why don't you let me go back in there and face the peril?

LAUNCELOT: It's too perilous.

They are right outside the castle by now.

GALAHAD: Look, it's my duty as a knight to try and sample as much peril as I can.

LAUNCELOT: No, no, we must find the Grail.

The thunderstorm is over. A bunch (sic) of PAGES *are tethered to a tree with more* MEN *waiting. Their tethers are untied and the* PAGES *start banging away with their coconuts.* GALAHAD *is swept along with them as they ride off.*

GALAHAD: Oh, let me go and have a bit of peril.

LAUNCELOT: No. It's unhealthy.

GALAHAD: . . . I bet you're gay.

GAWAIN *or* CONCORDE *gives a knowing glance at* LAUNCELOT. VOICE *comes in as they ride off.*

VOICE-OVER: Sir Launcelot had saved Galahad from almost
certain temptation but they were still lost, far from the
goal of their search for the Holy Grail. Only Bedevere
and King Arthur himself, riding day and night, had
made any progress.

16. ANIMATION/LIVE ACTION.
ARTHUR *and* BEDEVERE *in the depths of a dark forest with an
old blind* SOOTHSAYER. *He lies in a broken-down old
woodman's hut.*

ARTHUR: And this 'Enchanter' of whom you speak, he has
seen the Grail?
The SOOTHSAYER *laughs forbiddingly, adding to the
general spookiness of this encounter.*
ARTHUR: Where does he live? (*He stares into the blind eyes of
the* SOOTHSAYER.) Old man . . . where does he live . . .
SOOTHSAYER: He knows of a cave . . . a cave which no man
has entered.
ARTHUR: And . . . the Grail . . . the Grail is *there*?
The SOOTHSAYER *laughs again to himself.*
SOOTHSAYER: There is much danger . . . for beyond the cave
lies the Gorge of Eternal Peril which no man has ever
crossed.
ARTHUR: But the *grail* . . . where is the *grail*?
SOOTHSAYER: Seek you the Bridge of Death . . .
ARTHUR: The Bridge of Death? . . . which leads to the Grail.
*The old man laughs sinisterly and mockingly. They look
down and he is gone. They stand up. Suddenly behind them
is a noise. They turn sharply. In the door of the little hut is a
cat. It miaows and is gone. They slowly back out of the hut.
As they touch the doorposts they just flake away into dust.
The whole hut is rotten. It collapses.*

Spooky music. They are thoroughly shaken, and they begin to hear noises of people moving in the forest around them. They start to back cautiously away from the hut, suddenly there is a heavy footfall behind them. They turn in fear and:

Sudden cut to big close-up of a frightening black-browed evil face.

TALL KNIGHT OF NI: Ni!

ARTHUR and BEDEVERE recoil in abject fear. PATSY rears up with coconuts.

ARTHUR (*to* PATSY): Easy . . . boy, easy . . .

ARTHUR peers into the darkness.

Who are you?

SIX VOICES FROM DARKNESS: Ni! . . . Peng! . . . Neeee . . . Wom!

An extraordinary TALL KNIGHT in all black (possibly John with Mike on his shoulders) walks out from the dark trees. He is extremely fierce and of gruesome countenance. He walks towards KING ARTHUR and PATSY, who are wazzing like mad. (Salopian slang, meaning very scared, almost to the point of wetting oneself, e.g. before an important football match or prior to a postering. Salopian slang meaning a beating by the school praeposters. Sorry about the Salopian slant to this stage direction – Ed.)

ARTHUR (*wazzed stiff*): Who are you?

TALL KNIGHT: We are the Knights Who Say 'Ni'!

BEDEVERE: No! Not the Knights Who Say 'Ni'!

TALL KNIGHT: The same . . .

ARTHUR: Who are they?

TALL KNIGHT: We are the keepers of the Sacred Words. Ni . . . Peng . . . and Neee . . . Wom!

BEDEVERE: Those who hear them seldom live to tell the tale.

TALL KNIGHT: The Knights Who Say 'Ni'! demand a sacrifice.

ARTHUR (*to the* TALL KNIGHT): Knights Who Say 'Ni' . . .
we are but simple travellers. We seek the Enchanter who
lives beyond this wood and who . . .

TALL KNIGHT: Ni!

ARTHUR (*recoiling*): Oh!

TALL KNIGHT: Ni! Ni!

ARTHUR (*he cowers in fear*): Oh!

TALL KNIGHT: We shall say Ni! again if you do not appease us.

ARTHUR: All right! What do you want?

TALL KNIGHT: We want . . . a shrubbery!

ARTHUR: A *what*?

TALL KNIGHT: Ni! Ni! Ni . . . Peng . . . Nee . . . wum!
The PAGES *rear and snort and rattle their coconuts.*

ARTHUR: All right! All right! . . . no more, please. We will
find you a shrubbery . . .

TALL KNIGHT: You must return here with a shrubbery or
else . . . you shall not pass through this wood alive!

ARTHUR: Thank you, Knights Who Say Ni! You are fair and
just. We will return with a shrubbery.

TALL KNIGHT: One that looks nice.

ARTHUR: Of course

TALL KNIGHT: And not too expensive.

ARTHUR: Yes . . .

TALL KNIGHT: Now – go!

ARTHUR *and* BEDEVERE *turn and ride off.*

OTHER KNIGHTS: Ni! Ni!

Shouts of 'Ni' and 'Peng' ring behind them.

17. EXT. DAY.
Cut back to the HISTORIAN *lying in the glade. His* WIFE, *who has
been kneeling beside him, rises as two* POLICE PATROLMEN *enter
the glade. They bend over her* HUSBAND. *One takes out a notebook.*
Cut to an animated title: '*The Tale of Sir Launcelot*'.

18. INT. PRINCE'S ROOM IN CASTLE. DAY.

A young, quite embarrassingly unattractive PRINCE *is gazing out of a castle window. His* FATHER *stands beside him. He is also looking out. The* PRINCE *wears a long white undershirt (like a nightshirt).*

FATHER: One day, lad, all this will be yours . . .

PRINCE: What – the curtains?

FATHER: No! Not the curtains, lad . . . all that . . . (*Indicates the vista from the window.*) all that you can see, stretched out over the hills and valleys . . . as far as the eye can see and beyond . . . that'll be your kingdom, lad.

PRINCE: But, Mother . . .

FATHER: Father, lad.

PRINCE: But, Father, I don't really want any of that.

FATHER: Listen, lad, I built this kingdom up from nothing. All I had when I started was swamp . . . other kings said I was daft to build a castle on a swamp, but I built it all the same . . . just to show 'em. It sank into the swamp. So I built another one . . . that sank into the swamp. I built another one . . . that fell over and *then* sank into the swamp . . . So I built another . . . and that stayed up. . . . And that's what you're going to get, lad: the most powerful kingdom in this island.

PRINCE: But I don't want any of that, I'd rather . . .

FATHER: Rather what?

PRINCE: I'd rather . . . just . . . sing . . .
Music intro.

FATHER: You're not going into a song while I'm here!
Music stops.
Listen, lad, in twenty minutes you're going to be married to a girl whose father owns the biggest tract of open land in Britain . . .

PRINCE: I don't want land.

FATHER: Listen, Alice . . .

PRINCE: Herbert.

FATHER: Herbert . . . We built this castle on a bloody swamp, we need all the land we can get.

PRINCE: I don't like her.

FATHER: Don't like her? What's wrong with her? She's beautiful . . . she's rich . . . she's got huge tracts of land . . .

PRINCE: I know . . . but . . . I want the girl that I marry to have . . . a certain . . . special . . . something . . .

Music intro for song.

FATHER: Cut that out!

Music cuts off abruptly.

You're marrying Princess Lucky, so you'd better get used to the idea! Guards!

TWO GUARDS *enter and stand to attention on either side of the door. One of them has hiccoughs and does so throughout.*

FATHER: Make sure the Prince doesn't leave this room until I come and get him.

FIRST GUARD: Not . . . to leave the room . . . even if you come and get him.

FATHER: No. *Until* I come and get him.

SECOND GUARD: Hic.

FIRST GUARD: Until you come and get him, we're not to enter the room.

FATHER: No . . . You stay in the room and make sure he doesn't leave.

FIRST GUARD: . . . and you'll come and get him.

SECOND GUARD: Hic.

FATHER: That's right.

FIRST GUARD: We don't need to do anything apart from just stop him entering the room.

FATHER: Leaving the room.

FIRST GUARD: Leaving the room . . . yes.

FATHER: Got it?

SECOND GUARD: Hic.

FATHER makes to leave.

FIRST GUARD: Er . . . if . . . we . . . er . . .

FATHER: Yes?

FIRST GUARD: If we . . . er . . . (*Trying to remember what he was going to say.*)

FATHER: Look, it's simple. Just stay here and make sure he doesn't leave the room.

SECOND GUARD: Hic.

FATHER: Right?

FIRST GUARD: Oh, I remember . . . can he . . . er . . . can he leave the room *with* us?

FATHER (*carefully*): No . . . keep him in here . . . and make sure he doesn't . . .

FIRST GUARD: Oh, yes! We'll keep him in here, obviously. But if he *had* to leave . . . and we were with him.

FATHER: No . . . just keep him in here.

FIRST GUARD: Until you, or anyone else . . .

FATHER: No. Not anyone else – just me.

FIRST GUARD: Just you . . .

SECOND GUARD: Hic.

FIRST GUARD: Get back.

FATHER: Right.

FIRST GUARD: Okay. Fine. We'll remain here until you get back.

FATHER: And make sure he doesn't leave.

FIRST GUARD: What?

FATHER: Make sure he doesn't leave.

FIRST GUARD: The Prince . . . ?

FATHER: Yes . . . make sure . . .

FIRST GUARD: Oh yes, of course! I thought you meant *him*! (*He points to the other* GUARD *and laughs to himself.*) . . .

you know it seemed a bit daft me having to guard him
when he's a guard . . .

FATHER: Is that clear?

SECOND GUARD: Hic.

FIRST GUARD: Oh, yes. That's quite clear. No problem.

FATHER *pulls open the door and makes to leave the room.*
The GUARDS *follow.*

FATHER (*to the* GUARDS): Where are you going?

FIRST GUARD: We're coming with you.

FATHER: No, I want you to stay here and make sure he
doesn't leave the room until I get back.

FIRST GUARD: Oh, I see, right.

They take up positions on either side of the door.

PRINCE: But, Father.

FATHER: Shut your noise, you, and get that suit on!

He points to a wedding suit on a table or chair. FATHER
throws one last look at the BOY *and turns, goes out and
slams the door.*

   The PRINCE *slumps on to window seat, looking forlornly
out of the window. Music intro to song . . .*

   The door flies open, the music cuts off and FATHER *pokes
his head in.*

FATHER: And NO SINGING!

SECOND GUARD: Hic.

FATHER (*as he goes out*): Go and have a drink of water.

FATHER slams the door again. The GUARDS *take up their
positions. The* PRINCE *gazes out of the window again . . .
sighs . . . thinks . . . a thought strikes him . . . he gets up,
crosses to his desk and scribbles a quick note and impales it
on an arrow . . . takes a bow down from the wall . . . and
fires the arrow out of the window.*

   He looks wetly defiant at the GUARDS, *who smile
pleasantly.*

19. EXT. A FOREST. DAY.

Cut to the middle of the forest. SIR LAUNCELOT *is riding along with a trusty servant,* CONCORDE.

LAUNCELOT: And . . . o v e r . . . we go!

> *He strides over a big tree trunk . . . his 'horse' does run-and-jump . . .*

LAUNCELOT (*enthusiastically*): Well taken, Concorde!

CONCORDE (*rattling the coconuts in appreciation*): Thank you, sir, most kind . . .

LAUNCELOT: And another!

> CONCORDE *misses a beat.*

Steady! Good . . . and the last one . . .

> CONCORDE *does the run-up with the coconuts. He does the break for the leap . . . there is a thwack.* LAUNCELOT *is waiting for the horse to land.*

CONCORDE: Message for you, sir.

> *He falls forward revealing the arrow with the note.*

LAUNCELOT: Concorde – speak to me.

> *He realises he might be in danger and so starts to crawl off . . . when he notices the note. He takes it out and reads it.*

LAUNCELOT (*reading*): 'To whoever finds this note – I have been imprisoned by my father who wishes me to marry against my will. Please please please please come and rescue me. I am in the Tall Tower of Swamp Castle.'

> LAUNCELOT'*s eyes light up with holy inspiration.*

LAUNCELOT: At last! A call! A cry of distress . . . (*He draws his sword, and turns to* CONCORDE.) Concorde! Brave Concorde . . . you shall not have died in vain.

CONCORDE: I'm not quite dead, sir . . .

LAUNCELOT (*a little deflated*): Oh, well . . . er, brave Concorde! You shall not have been fatally wounded in vain.

CONCORDE: I think I could pull through, sir.

52

LAUNCELOT: Good Concorde . . . stay here and rest awhile.
    He makes to leap off dramatically.
CONCORDE: I think I'll be all right to come with you, sir.
LAUNCELOT: I will send help, brave friend, as soon as I have
    accomplished the most daring, desperate adventure in
    this genre.
CONCORDE: Really, I feel fine, sir.
LAUNCELOT: Farewell, Concorde . . .
CONCORDE: It just seems silly . . . me lying here.
    LAUNCELOT *plunges off into the forest.*

20. EXT. CASTLE GATEWAY. DAY.
*Two hanging banners one each side of the gate with the
monogram: 'H & L'.*

    *Two sentries with spears . . . slightly weddingy . . . red ribbons
on their right sleeves. A little nosegay of flowers on the tips of the
spears. We can hear from inside revelry and celebration. Music.*

    We hear LAUNCELOT's *footsteps. The* TWO SENTRIES *are
watching him. One of them raises his hand.*

    LAUNCELOT *leaps into shot with a mighty cry and runs the*
GUARD *through and hacks him to the floor. Blood.
Swashbuckling music (perhaps).* LAUNCELOT *races through into
the castle screaming.*

SECOND SENTRY: Hey!
    He looks down at his mutilated comrade.

21. EXT. DAY.
Cut to inside of the castle grounds or courtyard.

    In the sunlight beautifully dressed WEDDING GUESTS *are
arriving. Converging on a doorway. A country dance in progress.*
    SIR LAUNCELOT *rushes towards them.*

54

*Cut to hand-held close-ups as he charges through the crowd,
hacking right and left à la Errol Flynn at all who come in his way.*

*He fights his way through the country dance. Blood. Shrieks.
Bemused looks of* GUESTS *— not horror so much as
uncomprehending surprise.*

Possibly Errol Flynn music.

One COUNTRY DANCER *is left holding just a hand.*

Right and left the GUESTS *crumple in pools of blood as he
fights his way through the door and into the main hall.*

22. INT. DAY.

Cut to interior of main hall. Sound of busy preparations. MEN
setting up huge hogsheads of wine. MEN *putting up last-minute
flower arrangements.* COOKS *bearing huge trays of food, pies,
sucking pigs, a swan, boar's head, etc.*

The BRIDE *being dressed by several* ATTENDANTS. FATHER
ordering SERVANTS *around — organising the* STEWARDS, *etc.*

SIR LAUNCELOT *bursts through the middle of them, slashing
heroically, hacking, wounding and killing. Again fairly close-up
chaotic shots. We see* GUESTS *stagger back wounded — a* COOK
bites the dust, etc.

SIR LAUNCELOT *eventually reaches the staircase . . . runs up
it and into a small door.*

23. INT. DAY.

Cut to SIR LAUNCELOT *running up spiral staircase. He reaches
the door of the* PRINCE'*s room. He flings it open.*

FIRST GUARD: Ah! Now . . . we're not allowed to . . .

    SIR LAUNCELOT *runs him through, grabs his spear and
    stabs the other* GUARD *who collapses in heap. Hiccoughs
    quietly.*

SIR LAUNCELOT *runs to the window and kneels down in front of the* PRINCE, *averting his head.*

LAUNCELOT: Oh, fair one, behold your humble servant, Sir Launcelot, from the Court of Camelot. I have come to take you . . . (*He looks up for the first time and his voice trails away.*) away . . . I'm terribly sorry . . .

PRINCE: You got my note?

LAUNCELOT: Well . . . yes . . .

PRINCE: You've come to rescue me?

LAUNCELOT: Well . . . yes . . . but I hadn't realised . . .

PRINCE (*his eyes lighting up*): I knew someone would come. I knew . . . somewhere out there . . . there must be . . .
Music intro to song.

FATHER (*suddenly looking in at the door*): Stop that!
Music cuts out.

FATHER *sees* SIR LAUNCELOT *still kneeling before his son.*

FATHER: Who are you?

PRINCE: I'm . . . your son . . .

FATHER: Not *you*.

LAUNCELOT (*half standing self-consciously*): I'm . . . er . . . Sir Launcelot, sir.

PRINCE: He's come to rescue me, Father.

LAUNCELOT (*embarrassed*): Well, let's not jump to conclusions . . .

FATHER: Did you kill all those guards?

LAUNCELOT: Yes . . . I'm very sorry . . .

FATHER: They cost fifty pounds each!

LAUNCELOT: Well, I really am most awfully sorry but I . . . I can explain everything . . .

PRINCE: Don't be afraid of *him*, Sir Launcelot. I've got a rope here all ready . . .
He throws a rope out of the window which is tied to pillar in room. He looks rather pleased with himself that he has got it all ready.

FATHER: You killed eight wedding guests and all!

LAUNCELOT: Er, well . . . the thing is . . . I thought your son was a lady.

FATHER: I can understand that.

PRINCE (*half out of the window*): Hurry, brave Sir Launcelot.

FATHER (*to his* SON): Shut up! (*To* LAUNCELOT.) You only killed the bride's father – that's all –

LAUNCELOT: Oh dear, I didn't really mean to . . .

FATHER: Didn't mean to? You put your sword right through his head!

LAUNCELOT: Gosh – is he all right?

FATHER: You even kicked the bride in the chest! It's going to cost me a fortune!

LAUNCELOT: I can explain . . . I was in the forest . . . riding North from Camelot . . . when I got this note . . .

FATHER: Camelot? Are you from Camelot?

The PRINCE'*s head peeps over the windowsill.*

PRINCE: Hurry!

LAUNCELOT: I am, sir. I am a Knight of King Arthur.

FATHER: 'Mm . . . very nice castle, Camelot . . . very good pig country . . .

LAUNCELOT: Is it?

PRINCE (*out of vision*): I am ready, Sir Launcelot.

FATHER: Do you want to come and have a drink?

LAUNCELOT: Oh . . . that's awfully nice.

PRINCE (*out of vision, loud and shrill*): I am *ready!*

As they walk past the rope, the FATHER *nonchalantly cuts it with his knife. There is no sound except after a pause a slight squeal from very far away as the* PRINCE *makes contact with the ground.*

LAUNCELOT: It's just that when I'm in this genre, I tend to get over-excited and start to leap around and wave my sword about . . . and . . .

FATHER: Oh, don't worry about that . . . Tell me . . . doesn't

Camelot own that stretch of farmland up by the
mountains?

He puts his arm round LAUNCELOT's *shoulders as they go
through the door.*

24. INT. DAY.

Cut to the great hall. GUESTS *wounded and bloody, are tending
to the dead and injured, sighs and groans, the* PRINCESS *in her
white wedding dress is holding her chest and coughing blood.
People dabbing the stains off her dress.*

FATHER *and* SIR LAUNCELOT *start to walk down the grand
staircase. Talking to each other.*

One of the GUESTS *notices and points to* SIR LAUNCELOT.

GUEST: There he is!

As one man, all remaining able-bodied MEN *look up and
make for the staircase, muttering angrily.* SIR LAUNCELOT
grabs his sword.

FATHER: Hold it!

But it is too late. SIR LAUNCELOT *cannot be stopped. With
fearless abandon he throws himself into the* CROWD *and
starts hacking and slashing. He has carved quite a number
up before the* FATHER *can stop him and pulls him back on to
the stairs. Renewed groans and cries.*

FATHER (*shouting above the noise*): Hold it! *Please!*

LAUNCELOT: Sorry! . . . Sorry . . . (*With bitter self-reproach.*)
There you are you see . . . I just got excited again and I
get carried away . . . I'm ever so sorry. (*To the* CROWD.)
Sorry.

CROWD *kneeling round their wounded again. Moans, etc.*

GUEST: He's killed the best man!

LAUNCELOT: Oh, no . . .

Hostile shouts of 'arrest him', 'boom in shot', etc.

FATHER: Now hold it! This is Sir Launcelot from the Court of Camelot! He is a very brave and influential knight and my special guest today.

SECOND GUEST (*holding a limp* WOMAN): He's killed my auntie.

FATHER: No, please! This is meant to be a happy occasion! Let's not bicker and argue over who killed who . . . We are here to witness the union of two young people in the joyful bond of holy wedlock. Now unfortunately, one of them, my son Herbert, has just fallen to his death . . .
Murmurs from CROWD; *the* BRIDE *smiles with relief, coughs.*

But I don't want to think I've lost a son . . . as much as gained a daughter . . .
Smattering of applause.

For, since the tragic death of her father . . .

SHOUT FROM BACK: He's not quite dead!

FATHER: Since the fatal wounding of her father . . .

SHOUT FROM BACK: I think he's getting better!

FATHER *nods discreetly to a* SOLDIER *standing to one side. The* SOLDIER *slips off.* FATHER's *eyes watch him move round to where the voice came from.*

FATHER: For . . . since her own father . . . who . . . when he seemed about to recover . . . suddenly felt the icy . . . hand of death upon him.
A scuffle at the back.

SHOUT FROM BACK: Oh, he's died!

FATHER: I want his only daughter, from now onwards, to think of me as her old dad . . . in a very real and legally binding sense.
Applause.

And I'm sure . . . that the merger . . . er . . . the union . . . between the Princess and the brave but dangerous Sir Launcelot of Camelot . . .

LAUNCELOT: What?!

Gasp from the CROWD.

CROWD: The dead Prince!

There is CONCORDE *holding* 'THE DEAD PRINCE' *in his arms.*

CONCORDE: He's not *quite* dead!

PRINCE: I feel much better now.

FATHER: You fell out of the Tall Tower, you creep!

PRINCE: I was saved at the last minute.

FATHER: How?

PRINCE: Well . . . I'll tell you . . .

Music intro to song. CONCORDE *stands the* SON *on his feet and adopts cod 'and now a number from my friend' pose.*

FATHER: *Not* like that!

But the music doesn't stop and the CROWD *starts to sing.*

CROWD: He's going to tell.

FATHER: Shut up!

CROWD: He's going to tell . . .

FATHER (*screaming*): Shut UP!

As the music starts the FATHER *tries yelling at them and eventually gives up.* SIR LAUNCELOT *joins* CONCORDE *in the* CROWD.

CONCORDE: Quickly, sir, come this way!

LAUNCELOT: No! It's not right for my idiom. I must escape more . . . more . . .

CONCORDE: Dramatically, sir?

LAUNCELOT: Dramatically.

CROWD: He's going to tell

He's going to tell

He's going to tell about his great escape.

Oh he fell a long long way

But he's here with us today

What a wonderful . . . escape.

CONCORDE *goes.* SIR LAUNCELOT *runs back up the stairs,*

grabs a rope off the wall and swings out over the heads of the CROWD *in a swashbuckling manner towards a large window. He stops just short of the window and is left swinging pathetically back and forth.*

LAUNCELOT: Excuse me . . . could somebody give me a push . . .

25. EXT. A DESERTED VILLAGE. DUSK.

Toothless old CRONE *by the roadside.* ARTHUR *and* BEDEVERE *and two* PAGES *ride up and draw alongside the* CRONE.

ARTHUR: In this town is there anywhere where we can buy a shrubbery?

The OLD CRONE *crosses herself with a look of stark terror.*

CRONE: Who sent you?

ARTHUR: The Knights Who Say Ni!

CRONE: Aaaagh! (*She looks round in fear.*) No! We have no shrubberies here.

BEDEVERE: Surely, there must be.

ARTHUR: Listen, old crone! Unless you tell us where we can buy a shrubbery, my friend and I will . . . we will say 'Ni'!

CRONE: Do your worst!

ARTHUR: Very well, old crone. Since you will not assist us voluntarily . . . 'Ni'!

CRONE: No. Never. No shrubberies.

ARTHUR: Ni!

BEDEVERE: Nu!

ARTHUR: No. Ni! More like this. 'Ni'!

BEDEVERE: Ni, ni, ni!

ARTHUR: You're not doing it properly. Ni!

BEDEVERE: Ni!

ARTHUR: That's it. Ni! Ni!

A PASSER-BY *on a horse is observing them.*

ROGER: Are you saying 'Ni' to that old woman?

ARTHUR: Erm, yes.

ROGER: Oh, what sad times are these when passing ruffians can say 'Ni' at will to old ladies. There is a pestilence upon this land! Nothing is sacred. Even those who arrange and design cosmetic shrubberies are under considerable economic stress at this point in time.

ARTHUR: Did you say shrubberies?

ROGER: Yes. Shrubberies are my trade. I am a shrubber. My name is Roger the shrubber. I arrange, design and sell shrubberies.

BEDEVERE (*rather aggressively, to* ROGER): Ni!

ARTHUR: No. No. No!

26. EXT. GLADE. DUSK.
Cut to the glade in the forest again.

ARTHUR: Oh, Knights of Ni, here is your shrubbery. May we go now?

TALL KNIGHT: That is a good shrubbery. I like the laurels particularly – but there is one small problem.

ARTHUR: What is that?

TALL KNIGHT: We are no longer the Knights Who Say Ni!

OTHERS: No! Not at all . . .

ONE KNIGHT: Ni!

OTHERS: Sh!

ONE KNIGHT (*whispers*): Sorry.

TALL KNIGHT: We are now the Knights Who Go Neeeow . . . Wum . . . Ping!

OTHERS: Ni!

OTHERS: Ni!

ONE KNIGHT: Peng!

OTHERS: Ni!

64

OTHERS: Sh! Sh!

TALL KNIGHT: Therefore . . . we are no longer contractually bound by any agreements previously entered into by the Knights Who Say Ni!

ONE KNIGHT: Ni!

ANOTHER: Peng!

ANOTHER: Sh!

TALL KNIGHT: Shut up! (*To* ARTHUR.) Therefore we must give you a Test, a Test to satisfy the Knights Who Say Neeow . . . Wum . . . Ping!

OTHERS (*terrific chorus*): Ni! Ni! Peng Nee-wum!

ARTHUR: What is the Test, Knights of N . . . (*Can't say it.*) . . . recently Knights of Ni!

KNIGHT: Ni!

TALL KNIGHT: Firstly. You must get us another shrubbery!

OTHER KNIGHTS (*half seen*): More shrubberies! More shrubberies for the ex-Knights of Ni!

ARTHUR: Not *another* shrubbery –

TALL KNIGHT: When you have found another shrubbery, place the shrubbery here, beside *this* shrubbery . . . only slightly higher, so you get the two-level effect with a path through the middle.

OTHER KNIGHTS: A path! A little path for the late Knights of Ni!

Chorus of 'Ni! Ni!'.

TALL KNIGHT: When you have found the shrubbery, then you must cut down the mightiest tree in the forest . . . with a herring.

OTHER KNIGHTS: Yes! With a herring! With a herring! Cut down with a herring!

ARTHUR: We shall do *no* such thing . . . let us pass!

TALL KNIGHT: Oh, please.

ARTHUR: Cut down a tree with a herring? It can't be done.

OTHER KNIGHTS (*they all recoil in horror*): Oh!

TALL KNIGHT: Don't say that word!

ARTHUR: What word?

TALL KNIGHT: The word you just said.

ARTHUR: Which one?

TALL KNIGHT: I cannot tell you. Suffice to say is one of the words the Knights of Ni! cannot hear!

ARTHUR: How can we *not* say the word, if you don't tell us what it is?

TALL KNIGHT (*cringing in fear*): You said it again!

ARTHUR: What, 'is'?

TALL KNIGHT (*dismissively*): No, no . . . not 'is'!

OTHER KNIGHTS: Not '*is*'! Not '*is*'!

Suddenly singing is heard from deep in the forest.

SIR ROBIN'S SINGERS: Bravely good Sir Robin was not at all afraid/To have his eyeballs skewered . . .

TALL KNIGHT (*irritated*): 'Is' is all right . . . You wouldn't get far not saying 'is'!

BEDEVERE: My Liege, it's Sir Robin!

TALL KNIGHT (*covering his ears*): You've said the word *again*!

SIR ROBIN *and his* SINGERS *appear in the clearing. The* SINGERS *are going on cheerfully as usual and* ROBIN *walks in front of them, continually embarrassed at their presence.*

SINGERS: . . . and his kidneys burned and his nipples skewered off . . .

ROBIN *holds his hand up for silence.*

ARTHUR: Sir Robin!

He shakes his hand warmly.

ROBIN: My Liege! It's good to have found you again . . .

TALL KNIGHT: Now *he's* said the word!

ARTHUR: Where are you going, good Sir Robin?

ROBIN'S SINGERS: (*starting up again*) He was going home . . . he was giving up, he was throwing in the sponge.

ROBIN (*to* SINGERS): Shut up! No . . . er . . . no . . . I . . . er, I . . . er . . . I certainly wasn't giving up . . . I was actually looking for the Grail . . . er thing . . . in this forest.

ARTHUR: No . . . it lies beyond this forest.

TALL KNIGHT: Stop saying the word!

OTHER KNIGHTS: Stop saying the word! The word we cannot hear! The word . . .

ARTHUR (*losing his patience with the fearful* KNIGHTS OF 'NI'): Oh, stop it!

Terrific confusion amongst the KNIGHTS OF 'NI', *they roll on the ground covering their ears. The* TALL KNIGHT *remains standing, trying to control his* MEN.

OTHER KNIGHTS: They're *all* saying the word . . .

TALL KNIGHT: Stop saying it. AAAArghh! I've said it . . .

OTHER KNIGHTS: You've said it! Aaaaarghhh! . . . *we've* said it . . . we're all saying it.

ARTHUR *beckons to* BEDEVERE *and* ROBIN *and they pick their way through the helpless* KNIGHTS OF 'NI' *and away into the forest.*

27. EXT. HISTORIAN'S GLADE. DAY.
We cut to an almost subliminal shot of the HISTORIAN'S WIFE *being shown into a police car, which then roars off out of the glade.*

28. EXT. BEYOND THE FOREST. DAY. ANIMATION.
Shots of ARTHUR *etc. riding out of the forest. They leave the forest and meet* LAUNCELOT *and* GALAHAD.

VOICE-OVER: And so Arthur and Bedevere and Sir Robin set out on their search to find the Enchanter of whom the old man had spoken in scene twenty-four. Beyond the forest they met Launcelot and Galahad, and there was much rejoicing.

29. EXT. ANOTHER LANDSCAPE. DAY. ANIMATION.

VOICE-OVER: In the frozen land of Nador, they were forced to eat Robin's minstrels . . . and there was much rejoicing . . . A year passed . . .
Montage of shots of the KNIGHTS.
Autumn changed into Winter . . . Winter changed into Spring . . . Spring changed back into Autumn and Autumn gave Winter and Spring a miss and went straight on into Summer . . . Until one day . . .

30. EXT. WASTES. DAY.
The KNIGHTS *are riding along the top of a ridge. The country is wild and inhospitable. Suddenly some of them see fire in the distance and ride towards it. As they approach they see an impressive* WIZARD *figure striding around conjuring up fire from the ground and causing various bushes and branches to burst into flame.*

ARTHUR: What manner of man are you that can conjure up fire without flint or tinder?
TIM: I am an enchanter.
ARTHUR *looks at* BEDEVERE.
ARTHUR: By what name are you known?
TIM: There are some who call me Tim.
ARTHUR: Greetings, Tim the Enchanter!
TIM: Greetings, King Arthur.
ARTHUR: You know my name.
TIM: I do. (*Does another fire trick.*) You seek the Holy Grail.

69

Murmur of astonishment from the KNIGHTS.

ARTHUR: That is our quest. You know much that is hidden, O Tim.

TIM (*does another fire trick*): Quite.

Ripple of applause from the KNIGHTS.

ARTHUR: Yes, we seek the Holy Grail. (*Clears throat very quietly.*) Our quest is to find the Grail.

ONE OR TWO KNIGHTS: Yes, it is.

ARTHUR: And so we're looking for it.

KNIGHTS: Yes, we are.

BEDEVERE: We have been for some time.

KNIGHTS: Yes.

ROBIN: Months.

ARTHUR: Yes . . . and obviously any help we get is . . . is very . . . helpful.

GALAHAD: Do you know where it . . .

TIM *does another fire trick.*

ALL OTHER KNIGHTS: Sssssh!

ARTHUR: Fine . . . well, er . . . we mustn't take up any more of your time . . . I don't suppose . . . sorry to sort of keep on about it . . . you haven't by any chance . . . aaah . . . any idea where one might find . . . a . . . aaa . . .

TIM: What?

ARTHUR: A g . . . g . . . g . . .

TIM: A grail?

They all jump slightly and look about apprehensively.

ARTHUR: Er . . . yes . . . I think so.

ALL OTHER KNIGHTS: Yes

TIM: Yes.

ARTHUR: Fine.

ROBIN: Splendid!

OTHERS: Yes, marvellous.

TIM *looks thoughtful and they all stand around a little.*
Then TIM *produces another fire trick producing several*

different colours.

ARTHUR: Look, you're a busy man . . .

TIM: Yes, I can help you with your quest.

Slight pause.

ALL OTHER KNIGHTS: Thank you. Yes, thank you very much.

TIM: To the north there lies a cave, the Cave of Caerbannog, wherein, carved in mystic runes, upon the very living rock, the last words of Olfin Bedwere of Rheged . . .

There is a thunderclap and a wind starts. The KNIGHTS *get nervous.*

TIM: . . . make plain the resting place of the most Holy Grail.

ARTHUR: How shall we find this cave, O Tim?

TIM: Follow!

The KNIGHTS *register delight and wheel round on themselves.* But follow only if you are men of valour. For the entrance to this cave is guarded by a monster, a creature so foul and cruel that no man yet has fought with it and lived. Bones of full fifty men lie strewn about its lair . . . therefore, sweet knights, if you may doubt your strength or courage come no further, for death awaits you all with nasty big teeth.

ARTHUR: What an eccentric performance!

31. EXT. DAY.

Cut to impressive rock face with caves in it. The KNIGHTS *are 'riding' towards it. A foreboding atmosphere supervenes.* TIM *gives a signal for quietness.* ARTHUR *shushes the 'horses'.*

ARTHUR: Shhh!

The PAGES *decrease the amount of noise they are making with the coconuts for a few seconds. Then there is a burst of noise from them including whinnying.*

BEDEVERE (*to* ARTHUR): They're nervous, sire.

ARTHUR: Then we'd best leave them here and carry on on foot.

TIM takes a strange look at them. They walk on leaving the PAGES *behind. After a few more strides* TIM *halts them with a sign.*

TIM: Behold the Cave of Caerbannog!

Cut to shot of cave. Bones littered around. The KNIGHTS *get the wind up partially. A little dry ice, glowing green, can be seen at the entrance. Suddenly we become aware of total silence. Any noises the* KNIGHTS *make sound very exaggerated. They unsheathe their swords.*

ARTHUR: Keep me covered.

Stir among the KNIGHTS.

BEDEVERE: What with?

ARTHUR: Just keep me covered.

TIM: Too late.

ARTHUR: What?

TIM: There he is.

They all turn, and see a large white RABBIT *lollop a few yards out of the cave. Accompanied by a terrifying chord and jarring metallic monster noise.*

ARTHUR: Where?

TIM: There.

ARTHUR: Behind the rabbit?

TIM: It is the rabbit.

ARTHUR: . . . You silly sod.

TIM: What?

ARTHUR: You got us all worked up.

BEDEVERE: You cretin!

TIM: That is not an ordinary rabbit . . . 'tis the most foul cruel and bad-tempered thing you ever set eyes on.

ROBIN: You tit. I soiled my armour I was so scared.

TIM: That rabbit's got a vicious streak. It's a killer.

72

GALAHAD: Get stuffed.

TIM: He'll do you up a treat, mate.

GALAHAD: Oh yeah?

ROBIN: You mangy Scots git!

TIM: Look. I'm warning you.

ROBIN: What's he do? Nibble your bum?

TIM: Well, it's got huge . . . very sharp . . . it can jump a . . . look at the bones.

ARTHUR: Go on, Bors, chop its head off.

BORS: Right. Silly little bleeder. One rabbit stew coming up.

ARTHUR: Now look here, O Tim.

TIM: Look!

As TIM *points they all spin round to see the* RABBIT *leap at* BORS' *throat with an appalling scream. From a distance of about twenty feet there is a tin-opening noise, a cry from* BORS. *A quick close-up of a savage* RABBIT *biting through tin and* BORS' *head flies off. The* RABBIT *leaps back to the mouth of the cave and sits there looking at the* KNIGHTS' *direction and growling menacingly.*

ARTHUR: Je . . . sus Christ!

TIM: I warned you.

ROBIN: I done it again.

TIM: Did I tell you? Did you listen to me? Oh no, no, you knew better, didn't you. No, it's just an ordinary rabbit, isn't it. The names you called me. Well, don't say I didn't tell you.

ARTHUR: Oh, shut up.

TIM (*quietly*): It's always the same . . . if I've said it once.

ARTHUR: Charge!

They all charge with swords drawn towards the RABBIT. *A tremendous twenty-second fight with Peckinpahish shots and borrowing heavily also on the kung fu- and karate-type films ensues, in which some four* KNIGHTS *are comprehensively killed.*

Run away! Run away!

ALL KNIGHTS (*taking up the cry*): Run away! Run away!

They run down from the cave and hide, regrouping behind some rocks. TIM, *some way away, is pointing at them and laughing derisively.*

TIM: Ha ha ha. Ha ha ha.

ARTHUR: Who did we lose?

LAUNCELOT: Sir Gawain.

GALAHAD: Ector.

ARTHUR: And Bors. Five.

GALAHAD: *Three*, sir!

ARTHUR: Well, we'll not risk another frontal assault. That rabbit's dynamite.

ROBIN: Would it help to confuse him if we ran away more?

ARTHUR: Shut up. Go and change your armour.

ROBIN leaves, walking strangely.

GALAHAD: Let us taunt it. It may become so cross it will make a mistake.

ARTHUR: Like what?

GALAHAD cannot find a suitable answer to this.

GALAHAD: Do we have any bows?

ARTHUR: No.

BEDEVERE: We have the Holy Hand Grenade.

ROBIN: The what?

BEDEVERE: The Holy Hand Grenade of Antioch. 'Tis one of the sacred relics Brother Maynard always carries with him.

ALL: Yes. Of course.

ARTHUR (*shouting*): Bring up the Holy Hand Grenade!

Slight pause. Then from the area where the 'HORSES' are, a small group of MONKS process forward towards the KNIGHTS, the leading MONK bearing an ornate golden reliquary, and the accompanying MONKS chanting and waving incense. They reach the KNIGHTS. The hand grenade is suffused with the holy glow.

ARTHUR *takes it. Pause.*

ARTHUR: How does it . . . er . . .

LAUNCELOT: I know not.

ARTHUR: Consult the Book of Armaments.

BROTHER MAYNARD: Armaments Chapter Two Verses Nine to Twenty-One.

ANOTHER MONK (*reading from Bible*): And St Attila raised the hand grenade up on high saying, 'O Lord, bless this Thy hand grenade that with it Thou mayest blow Thine enemies to tiny bits, in Thy mercy' and the Lord did grin and the people did feast upon the lambs and sloths and carp and anchovies and orang-utangs and breakfast cereals and fruit bats and . . .

BROTHER MAYNARD: Skip a bit, brother . . .

ANOTHER MONK: . . . Er . . . oh, yes . . . and the Lord spake, saying, 'First shalt thou take out the Holy Pin, then shalt thou count to three, no more, no less. Three shall be the number thou shalt count, and the number of the counting shall be three. Four shalt thou not count neither count thou two, excepting that thou then proceed to three. Five is right out. Once the number three, being the third number, be reached then lobbest thou thy Holy Hand Grenade of Antioch towards thy foe, who being naughty in my sight, shall snuff it.

ARTHUR: Right.

He pulls pin out. The MONK *blesses the grenade as . . .*

ARTHUR (*quietly*): One, two, five . . .

GALAHAD: *Three*, sir!

ARTHUR: Three.

ARTHUR *throws the grenade at the* RABBIT. *There is an explosion and cheering from the* KNIGHTS.

ALL KNIGHTS: Praise be to the Lord. Huzzah!

32. INT. CAVE. DAY.

Mix through to the KNIGHTS *entering the cave. It is a large cave and as they walk inside it we see in the darkness at the side of the cave a fearsome-looking* CREATURE *which watches them with some surprise as they walk to some writing carved on the back of the cave wall. The* KNIGHTS *are accompanied by* BROTHER MAYNARD.

ARTHUR: There! Look!

BEDEVERE: What does it say?

ARTHUR: What language is this?

BEDEVERE: Brother Maynard, you are a scholar.

BROTHER MAYNARD: It is Aramaic.

GALAHAD: Of course. Joseph of Arimathea!

ALL: Of course.

ARTHUR: What does it say, Brother?

BROTHER MAYNARD: It reads . . . 'Here may be found the last words of Joseph of Arimathea.'
Excitement.
'He who is valorous and pure of heart may find the Holy Grail in the aaaaarrrrrrggghhh . . .'

ARTHUR: What?

BROTHER MAYNARD: 'The aaaaaarrrrrrggghhh . . .'

BEDEVERE: What's that?

BROTHER MAYNARD: He must have died while carving it.

BEDEVERE: Oh, come on.

BROTHER MAYNARD: That's what it says.

ARTHUR (*miming*): But if he was dying he wouldn't bother to carve 'aaaaaarrrrrrggghhh'. He'd just say it.

BROTHER MAYNARD: It's down there carved in stone.

GALAHAD: Perhaps he was dictating.

ARTHUR: Shut up. Is that all it says?

BROTHER MAYNARD: That's all. 'Aaaaaarrrrrrggghhh.'

ARTHUR: 'Aaaaaarrrrrrggghhh.'

BEDEVERE: Do you think he meant the Camargue?

GALAHAD: Where's that?

BEDEVERE: France, I think.

LAUNCELOT: Isn't there a St Aaaaaarrrrrrggghhh's in
    Cornwall?

ARTHUR: No, that's St Ives.

A muffled roar is heard.

BEDEVERE: Oooooh!

LAUNCELOT: No, 'Aaaaaarrrrrrggghhh . . .' at the back of
    the throat.

BEDEVERE: No! 'Ooooh!' in surprise and alarm!

*He indicates the entrance of the cave. They all turn and look.
There in the opening is a huge, unpleasant, fairly well-
drawn cartoon beast.*

ARTHUR: Oh!

GALAHAD: My God!

LAUNCELOT: What is it?

BEDEVERE: I know! I know! I know!

ARTHUR: What?

BEDEVERE: It's the . . . oh . . . (*Snaps his fingers as he tries to
    remember.*) it's the . . . it's on the tip of my tongue . . .

Another hideous roar.

    That's it!

ARTHUR: What?

BEDEVERE: It's The Legendary Black Beast of Arrrghhh!

VOICE OVER THE ANIMATION: As the horrendous black
    beast lunged forward, escape for Arthur and his knights
    seemed hopeless, when suddenly . . . the animator
    suffered a fatal heart attack.

ANIMATOR: Aaaaagh!

VOICE: The cartoon peril was no more . . . the quest for the
    Holy Grail could continue.

They run off. Darkness. The MONSTER *lumbering through
on animation.*

*Animated sequence. Leads through to the group
reappearing and seeing a distant opening to the cave. They
reach the opening. It is day.*

33. EXT. DAY.

*The KNIGHTS emerge from the mouth of the cave to find
themselves in a breathtaking, barren landscape. Glencoe. They
are half the way up the side of a mountain. They rest a few
seconds and get their breath back.*

GALAHAD: There it is!

ARTHUR: The Bridge of Death!

ROBIN (*to himself*): Oh! Great . . .

BEDEVERE: Look! It's the old man from scene twenty-four –
what's he doing here?

ARTHUR: He is the Keeper of the Bridge. He asks each
traveller five questions . . .

GALAHAD: Three questions.

ARTHUR: Three questions . . . He who answered the five
questions . . .

GALAHAD: Three questions.

ARTHUR: Three questions, may cross in safety.

ROBIN: And what if you get a question wrong?

ARTHUR: You are cast into the Gorge of Eternal Peril.

ROBIN: Oh . . . wacko!

GALAHAD: Who's going to answer the questions?

ARTHUR: Sir Robin, brave Sir Robin, you go.

ROBIN: Hey! I've got a great idea! Why doesn't Sir Launcelot
go?

LAUNCELOT: Yes. Let me. I will take it single-handed . . . I
will make a feint to the north-east . . .

ARTHUR: No, hang on! Just answer the five questions . . .

GALAHAD: Three questions.

ARTHUR: Three questions . . . and we will watch and
pray . . .

LAUNCELOT: I understand, my Liege.

ARTHUR: Good luck, brave Sir Launcelot . . . God be with
you.

LAUNCELOT *approaches the* BRIDGEKEEPER.

BRIDGEKEEPER: Stop!

LAUNCELOT *stops. The* KNIGHTS *watch anxiously.*
ARTHUR *sniffs briefly and glances momentarily down at*
ROBIN's *lower armour.*

BRIDGEKEEPER: Who approacheth the Bridge of Death
Must answer me
These questions three!
Ere the other side he see!

LAUNCELOT: Ask me the questions, Bridgekeeper. I am not
afraid.

BRIDGEKEEPER: What is your name?

LAUNCELOT: My name is Launcelot.

BRIDGEKEEPER: What is your quest?

LAUNCELOT: To find the Holy Grail.

BRIDGEKEEPER: What is your favourite colour?

LAUNCELOT: Blue.

BRIDGEKEEPER: All right. Off you go.

SIR LAUNCELOT *runs across into the mist. The bridge
perhaps disappears into the mist and we cannot see the other
side.* ARTHUR *and* ROBIN *exchange glances.* ROBIN *breathes
a great sigh of relief.*

ROBIN: That's *easy!*

A pause and then a slightly undignified rush for the bridge.
ARTHUR *remains behind a bit.* ROBIN *reaches the bridge
first.*

BRIDGEKEEPER: Stop!
Who approacheth the Bridge of Death
Must answer me

These questions three!

Ere the other side he see!

ROBIN: Ask me the questions, Bridgekeeper. I am not afraid.

The eager KNIGHTS *behind* ROBIN *wrinkle their noses slightly and fall back a little.*

BRIDGEKEEPER: What is your name?

ROBIN: My name is Sir Robin of Camelot!

BRIDGEKEEPER: What is your quest?

ROBIN: I seek the Grail!

BRIDGEKEEPER: What is the capital of Assyria?

ROBIN (*indignantly*): I don't know *that!*

He is immediately hurled by some unseen force over the edge of the precipice.

ROBIN: Aaaaaaaaaaaargh!

34. EXT. DAY.

Cut to SIR LAUNCELOT *who is only just arriving on the other side. He looks back across the invisible chasm. Dimly in the distance he hears:*

GAWAIN (*out of vision*): Sir Gawain of Camelot!

BRIDGEKEEPER (*out of vision*): What is your quest?

GAWAIN (*out of vision*): To seek the Holy Grail.

BRIDGEKEEPER: What is your favourite colour?

GAWAIN: Blue . . . no yellooooooww!

GAWAIN *is cast into the gorge.*

ARTHUR *and* BEDEVERE *step forward.*

BRIDGEKEEPER: What is your name?

ARTHUR: It is Arthur, King of the Britons.

BRIDGEKEEPER: What is your quest?

ARTHUR: To seek the Holy Grail.

BRIDGEKEEPER: What is the air-speed velocity of an unladen swallow?

ARTHUR: What do you mean? An African or a European
swallow?

BRIDGEKEEPER: Er . . . I don't know that . . . aaaagh!

BRIDGEKEEPER is cast into the gorge.

BEDEVERE: How do you know so much about swallows?

ARTHUR: Well, you have to know these things when you're a
king, you know.

*Suddenly they appear at water's edge. They look across the
water. A huge expanse disappearing into the mist. How can
they cross?*

*Suddenly the air is filled with ethereal music, and out of
the mist appears a wonderful barge silently and slowly
drifting towards them.*

*They gaze in wonder. The mysterious boat comes to where
they are standing. As if bewitched, they find themselves
drawing closer.*

35. EXT. DAY.

*The boat carries them across a magical lake. They land and get
out of the boat, their faces suffused with heavenly radiance, and
fall to their knees.*

Crescendo on music.

ARTHUR: God be praised! The deaths of many fine knights
have this day been avenged.

*Music swells. They bend their heads in prayer, before a
castle for which they have searched for so long. Suddenly a
voice comes from the battlements.*

Music cuts dead.

FROG: Ha ha! Hello! Smelly English K . . . niggets . . . and
Monsieur Arthur King, who has the brain of a duck, you
know.

The KNIGHTS look up.

FROG: We French persons outwit you a second time, perfidious English mousedropping hoarders . . . how you say: 'Begorrah!'

ARTHUR stands and shouts.

ARTHUR: How dare you profane this place with your presence! I command you, in the name of the Knights of Camelot, open the door to the Sacred Castle to which God himself has guided us! (*He turns to the* KNIGHTS.) Come.

ARTHUR and the KNIGHTS advance towards the castle.

FROG: How you English say: I one more time, mac, I unclog my nose towards you, sons of a window-dresser, so you think you could out-clever us French fellows with your silly knees-bent creeping about advancing behaviour. (*Blows a raspberry.*) I wave my private parts at your aunties, you brightly coloured, mealy-templed, cranberry-smelling, electric donkey-bottom biters.

By this time ARTHUR and BEDEVERE and GALAHAD have reached the door. ARTHUR bangs on the door.

ARTHUR: In the name of our Lord, we demand entrance to the Sacred Castle.

Jeering from the battlements.

FROG: No chance, English bed-wetting types. We burst our pimples at you, and call your door-opening request a silly thing. You tiny-brained wipers of other people's bottoms.

French laughter.

ARTHUR: If you do not open these doors, we will take the castle by force . . .

A bucket of slops lands on ARTHUR. He tries to retain his dignity.

ARTHUR: In the name of God . . . and the glory of our . . .

Another bucket of what can only be described as human ordure hits ARTHUR.

. . . Right! (*To the* KNIGHTS.) That settles it.

They turn and walk away. French jeering follows them.

FROG: Yes, depart a lot at this time, and cut the approaching any more or we fire arrows into the tops of your heads and make castanets of your testicles already.

ARTHUR (*to* KNIGHTS): Walk away. Just ignore him.

ARTHUR, BEDEVERE *and* GALAHAD *walk off. A small hail of chickens, watercress, badgers and mattresses follows them. But they are on their dignity as they try to talk nonchalantly as they walk away into the trees.*

FROG: And now remain gone, illegitimate-faced bugger-folk! And if you think you got a nasty time this taunting, you ain't heard nothing yet, dappy k . . . niggets, and A. King Esquire.

Cut back to ARTHUR *still walking away. French taunts still audible in the distance.*

FRENCH: You couldn't catch clap in a brothel, silly English K . . . niggets . . .

ARTHUR (*to* BEDEVERE): We shall attack at once.

BEDEVERE: Yes, my Liege. (*He turns.*) Stand by for attack!!

Cut to enormous army forming up. Trebuchets, rows of PIKEMEN, *siege towers, pennants flying, shouts of 'Stand by for attack!' Traditional army build-up shots. The shouts echo across the ranks of the army. We see various groups reacting, and stirring themselves in readiness.*

ARTHUR: Who are they?

BEDEVERE: Oh, just some friends!

We end up back with ARTHUR. *He seems satisfied that the* ARMY *is ready.*

Panning down the serried ranks, pikes ready, pennants flapping in the wind. Some of the horses whinny nervously, and rattle their coconuts.

ARTHUR *is satisfied at last. He addresses the castle.*

ARTHUR: French persons! Today the blood of many valiant

knights shall be avenged. In the name of God, we shall not stop our fight until each one of you lies dead and the Grail returns to those whom God has chosen.

ARTHUR *lowers his visor, turns to have a last look at* ARMY, *then:*

Charge!

The mighty ARMY *charges. Thundering noise of feet. Clatter of coconuts. Shouts etc.*

They charge towards the castle.

Suddenly there is the wail of a siren and a couple of police cars roar round in front of the charging ARMY *and the* POLICE *leap out and stop them.* TWO POLICEWOMEN *and the* HISTORIAN'S WIFE. *Black Marias skid up behind them.*

The ARMY *halts.*

HISTORIAN'S WIFE: They're the ones, I'm sure.

INSPECTOR END OF FILM: Grab 'em!

The POLICE *grab* ARTHUR *and bundle him into the Maria.* SIR BEDEVERE *is led off with a blanket over his head. The* KNIGHTS *are bundled into the Black Maria and the van drives off.*

The rest of the ARMY *stand around looking at a loss.*

INSPECTOR END OF FILM (*picks up megaphone*): All right! Clear off! Go on!

A few reaction shots of the ARMY *not quite sure what to do.*

INSPECTOR END OF FILM: Move along. There's nothing to see! Keep moving!

Suddenly he notices the cameras.

As the Black Maria drives away quick shot through window of all the KNIGHTS *huddled inside.*

INSPECTOR END OF FILM (*to camera*): All right, put that away, sonny.

He walks over to it and puts his hand over the lens.

The films runs out through the gate and the projector shines on the screen.

There is a blank screen for some fifteen seconds.
Slushy organ music starts and the houselights in the
cinema come on . . . organ music continues as the audience
leave.

Cast List

Graham Chapman played: KING ARTHUR, HICCOUGHING GUARD, THREE-HEADED KNIGHT

John Cleese played: SECOND SOLDIER WITH A KEEN INTEREST IN BIRDS, LARGE MAN WITH DEAD BODY, THE BLACK KNIGHT, MR NEWT (a village blacksmith interested in burning witches), A QUITE EXTRAORDINARILY RUDE FRENCHMAN, TIM THE WIZARD, SIR LAUNCELOT

Terry Gilliam played: PATSY (Arthur's trusty steed), THE GREEN KNIGHT, SOOTHSAYER, BRIDGEKEEPER, SIR GAWAIN (the first to be killed by the rabbit)

Eric Idle played: THE DEAD COLLECTOR, MR BLINT (a village ne'er-do-well very keen on burning witches), SIR ROBIN, THE GUARD WHO DOESN'T HICCOUGH BUT TRIES TO GET THINGS STRAIGHT, CONCORDE (Sir Launcelot's trusty steed), ROGER THE SHRUBBER (a shrubber), BROTHER MAYNARD

Neil Innes played: THE FIRST SELF-DESTRUCTIVE MONK, ROBIN'S LEAST FAVOURITE MINSTREL, THE PAGE CRUSHED BY A RABBIT, THE OWNER OF A DUCK

Terry Jones played: DENNIS'S MOTHER, SIR

Michael Palin played:	BEDEVERE, THREE-HEADED KNIGHT, PRINCE HERBERT FIRST SOLDIER WITH A KEEN INTEREST IN BIRDS, DENNIS, MR DUCK (a village carpenter who is almost keener than anyone else to burn witches), THREE-HEADED KNIGHT, SIR GALAHAD, KING OF SWAMP CASTLE, BROTHER MAYNARD'S ROOMMATE.
Connie Booth played:	THE WITCH
Carol Cleveland played:	ZOOT and DINGO
Bee Duffell played:	OLD CRONE TO WHOM KING ARTHUR SAID 'NI!'
John Young played:	THE DEAD BODY THAT CLAIMS IT ISN'T, AND THE HISTORIAN WHO ISN'T A.J.P. TAYLOR AT ALL
Rita Davies played:	THE HISTORIAN WHO ISN'T A.J.P. TAYLOR (honestly)'S WIFE
Sally Kinghorn played:	Either WINSTON or PIGLET
Avril Stewart played:	Either PIGLET or WINSTON